"*Tackling Tough Topics with Faith and Fiction* is full of help and hope for our Catholic youth and the adults who minister among them! Confronted daily with pressures, stresses, temptations, and media influences of a secularized culture, young people today want to know how to live their faith. This practical book provides adult leaders a step-by-step guide to introduce sensitive subjects and helps youth learn to follow Christ in the midst of the tough situations of their everyday lives. The Church needs resources of just this sort."

— *Archbishop Wilton D. Gregory, SLD, Archbishop of Atlanta*

"In a field rich with solid catechetical resources, I was never tempted to use the word 'genius'—until now. *Tackling Tough Topics with Faith and Fiction* by Diana Jenkins is extraordinary in its power and simplicity. With exceptional insight and a remarkably creative approach to sensitive subjects (for a hyper-sensitive audience), Jenkins's short, fictional, first-person stories expose and illuminate tough, timely issues without offending or threatening the dignity of the teen or young adult reader. Accompanying discussion questions, facts, activities, Scripture, and other resources are unified, coherent, and profoundly satisfying. Give us more resources like this one. Bravo!"

— *Lisa Mladinich, author,* Be an Amazing Catechist: Inspire the Faith of Children, *founder, AmazingCatechists.com*

TACKLING
TOUGH TOPICS

with Faith and Fiction

TACKLING
TOUGH TOPICS

with Faith and Fiction

By Diana R. Jenkins

Pauline
BOOKS & MEDIA
Boston

Library of Congress Cataloging-in-Publication Data

Jenkins, Diana R.
 Tackling tough topics with faith and fiction / By Diana R. Jenkins.
   pages cm
 ISBN-13: 978-0-8198-7495-5
 ISBN-10: 0-8198-7495-7
 1. Teenagers--Conduct of life--Study and teaching. 2. Christian ethics--Study and teaching. 3. Christian education of teenagers. 4. Fiction. I. Title.
 BJ1661.J46 2014
 268'.433--dc23

                    2013031286

The Scripture quotations contained herein are from the *New Revised Standard Version Bible: Catholic Edition*, copyright © 1989, 1993, Division of Christian Education of the National Council of the Churches of Christ in the United States of America. Used by permission. All rights reserved.

Excerpts from the English translation of the *Catechism of the Catholic Church* for use in the United States of America, copyright © 1994, United States Catholic Conference, Inc. — Libreria Editrice Vaticana. Used with permission.

Cover photo by Mary Emmanuel Alves, FSP
Cover and book design by Mary Joseph Peterson, FSP

Photo credits: Mary Emmanuel Alves, FSP—p. c, 1, 2, 3, 4, 10, 16, 22, 28, 34, 40, 46, 52, 58;
Mary Joseph Peterson, FSP—p. 6; © iStock Photo/RyanJLane—p. h, 12; © iStock Photo/jabejon—p. h, 18;
© iStock Photo/LindaYolanda—p. h, 24; © iStock Photo/Adam Filipowicz—p. 30; © iStock Photo/KathyDewar—p. 36;
© iStock Photo/Todd Taulman—p. 42; © iStock Photo/Btrenkel—p. h, 48; © iStock Photo/duncan1890—p. h, 54;
© iStock Photo/RusN—p. 60

Published by Pauline Books & Media, 50 Saint Pauls Avenue, Boston, MA 02130-3491

Printed in the U.S.A.

www.pauline.org

Pauline Books & Media is the publishing house of the Daughters of St. Paul, an international congregation of women religious serving the Church with the communications media.

1 2 3 4 5 6 7 8 9   18 17 16 15 14

Contents

How to Use This Book

Today's young teens will face many challenges before they reach adulthood, and they'll need faith to guide them along the way. But it's not easy for kids—or adults—to apply Catholic principles to real life when they're overwhelmed by temptations, peer pressure, media influences, stress, family issues, physical changes, society's problems, and a culture that is increasingly out-of-sync with Christian values. They need caring and wise adults to help them understand the relevance of their faith, and to encourage them to follow Christ even in the toughest situations.

Nobody wants to talk about tough issues, especially with kids and teens on the threshold of those most difficult—and awkward—years. But we all know that *somebody* has to begin the conversation. This book is intended to provide resources to equip teachers, catechists, parents, and anyone else who wants to tackle that job. Its ten chapters cover a number of sensitive topics: pornography, cyberbullying, modesty, being embarrassed by family, materialism, dishonesty, body image, pressure to achieve, depression, and substance abuse. The focal point of each chapter is a short story about a contemporary young teen dealing with a real life challenge to his or her faith.

Why fiction? Stories appeal to teens by *showing* how faith principles relate to real life instead of just *telling* or *preaching* about them. Because what characters encounter and how they respond can be completely controlled, stories can provide a nonthreatening way for adults to engage kids and help them examine sensitive issues. When young readers become involved in and entertained by fiction, they become open to its message.

Each chapter includes the following sections, all designed to assist the teacher's work with young teens:

The Facts

The statistics and other information in this section prepare the teacher to discuss the current chapter's issue. This information can be shared with students at the teacher's discretion.

Scripture and the Catechism

These connections are found in the teacher section of each chapter, but they can guide students, too.

The Story

The story should be previewed by the teacher to ensure its suitability for his/her students. Previewing can also help the teacher decide the most appropriate presentation. Stories can be read aloud by students, read aloud by the teacher, or read silently.

Tackling Tough Topics with Faith and Fiction is meant to be a flexible resource. Every chapter includes reproducible pages for the student and stands on its own so the chapters can be used in any order. Teachers may choose to present a few chapters that fit the needs and maturity level of their students, or they can work through the book as an entire program. (A reproducible parent letter about the program is available in the back of the book, along with other useful supplemental material.)

I hope this book helps you feel more comfortable and confident about opening up a conversation with today's kids about difficult subjects in the context of faith. May God bless you as you guide our young teens and help them grow their faith and live it more fully.

— *Diana R. Jenkins*

Discussion Questions

Thought-provoking questions lead students to engage the story and topic on a personal level and can be used for group discussion or used as a written assignment.

Activity

A wrap-up project appropriate to the current topic is included, but teachers can also choose from an appendix of other possible activities on page 64.

Prayer

A relevant prayer helps students engage the topic in the presence of God.

The Message

This section offers practical suggestions about how students can deal with the current chapter's issue.

INTERNET PORNOGRAPHY

THE ISSUE

THE FACTS

Studies show that 30–70 percent of kids come across Internet pornography accidentally. The statistics may vary, but they clearly point to a serious problem. Unintentional exposures most often occur during innocent searches, but kids can also inadvertently bring up pornography through pop-up ads, links on other websites, emails, and instant messages. (After accessing a pornographic website, a kid may find himself "mousetrapped"—unable to exit because whatever he does takes him to more sexual images or to similar sites.) Over half of the kids who experience accidental exposures never report what happened. Many are tempted to continue viewing pornography. Though pornography is often considered a male problem, studies reveal that nearly a third of Internet pornography consumers are female, and pornography addiction among women has increased in recent years.

SCRIPTURE

No testing has overtaken you that is not common to everyone. God is faithful, and he will not let you be tested beyond your strength, but with the testing he will also provide the way out so that you may be able to endure it.

1 Corinthians 10:13

"You have heard that it was said, 'You shall not commit adultery.' But I say to you that everyone who looks at a woman with lust has already committed adultery with her in his heart."

Matthew 5:27–28

CATECHISM

Pornography consists in removing real or simulated sexual acts from the intimacy of the partners, in order to display them deliberately to third parties. It offends against chastity because it perverts the conjugal act, the intimate giving of spouses to each other. It does grave injury to the dignity of its participants (actors, vendors, the public), since each one becomes an object of base pleasure and illicit profit for others. It immerses all who are involved in the illusion of a fantasy world. It is a grave offense. Civil authorities should prevent the production and distribution of pornographic materials.

CCC no. 2354

Get the Picture

It was an accident, OK? I'm really into cameras, and I was innocently surfing the web for photography tips. Maybe I misspelled something. Maybe I clicked the wrong link. I don't know what happened, but suddenly I was on a website that would make my mother freak.

Yeah, one of those. The girls had their hands or a sheet or something over the important parts, but you could tell they were naked.

I told myself I shouldn't be looking at pictures like that, but I went ahead and explored the site. When Mom's car pulled into the driveway, I quickly switched to my favorite site about creating special effects with your camera.

"Hi, Ryan." Mom stuck her head into my bedroom. "Homework done?"

"Um . . . not yet," I said.

She came in further—close enough to read the computer screen. "You and photography," she said, shaking her head. "Get to work, shutterbug."

"OK, OK!" I shuffled through some papers until I heard her leave. Then I collapsed on my desk with a sigh.

The next afternoon I went online to check out prices for zoom lenses. Usually I love doing that kind of thing even though it takes me forever to save up for camera equipment. But this time my mind kept wandering to yesterday's little discovery. Finally I gave in to temptation and returned to the site. But I didn't look at it for long. Ten minutes tops. Well, maybe an hour. When Mom got home, I changed back to the camera webstore.

That night I had trouble sleeping. I kept thinking about those naked girls and the more I thought about them the more I wanted to see them again, of course. When I couldn't take it any longer, I snagged my phone off the nightstand and went back to the website.

It didn't feel right to be looking at those photos, but I kept doing it anyway. I told myself plenty of other guys did the same thing. Really, what red-blooded male would pass up a chance like this? Maybe what I was doing wasn't so great, but at least it was perfectly normal.

I don't know how long I stayed on the site that night, but finally I quit and tried to get some sleep. But then I lay awake for hours, thinking about the photos and feeling disgusted with myself. I decided I was never doing that again. Never.

But when I woke up in the middle of the next night, I felt my phone pulling me like a magnet, and soon I was at it again. The next night, too. And the next. I kept telling myself I had to quit doing this stuff, but I went back to the site again and again over the next few weeks. And I found other pornographic sites, too. I figured there had to be thousands of them out there. How was anybody supposed to resist that kind of temptation?

One afternoon I couldn't even start my homework because I kept thinking about all those sites. Even though Mom could get home any minute, I grabbed my phone and surfed around, trying to find new sites, new photos, and new girls. I figured I'd exit as soon as I heard the car, but the next thing I knew footsteps were coming down the hall! I managed to escape in time, but Mom looked furious anyway as she marched into my room.

"What's wrong?" I asked, casually setting my phone aside.

"When I came home for lunch, I found this in the mail." She shook some papers at me. "It's the phone bill. And it's huge. Mostly because of our data plan."

My heart sank, but I tried to cling to the hope that I wasn't busted. "Wow," I said. "It sounds like they made some kind of mistake."

"That's what I thought," she said. "Until I called the company and found out you've been spending a lot of time online. In the middle of the night! What's going on?"

I couldn't think of a good answer to that question so I just shrugged.

She stuck out her hand. "Let me see your phone."

It didn't take her long to check my history and figure out what I'd been doing. At first she just seemed shocked as she followed my footsteps through the world of porn, but after a while she looked so sad I couldn't stand it.

"I'm sorry," I mumbled.

She plopped onto my bed. "Come here, Ryan," she said, her eyes still on my phone. "I want you to *really* look at this girl."

Like I wanted to look at a naked girl *with* my mother! "Mom, please . . . "

"Come here!" When I sat beside her, she held the phone toward me and said, "Look at her. Who do you think she is when she's not posing like this?"

I flicked my eyes at the photo, then away. "I . . . I don't know what you mean."

"Well," said Mom, "she has a life, doesn't she? And a family. And feelings. She's a real person."

Of course, I knew the girls in those pictures were real, but I had always been too busy staring at their bodies to think of them as actual people. I mean . . . I hardly even glanced at their faces! I turned and looked into the eyes of the girl in the photo. She was somebody's daughter or sister or cousin. Did her family know what she was doing? How did *they* feel about it?

And how did *she* feel? She was showing herself to people—like me!—people who didn't have any respect for her as a person. Didn't she realize that? And if she did, then where was her self-respect? It was depressing to think about how worthless she might feel, and even worse to realize that *I* had treated her as if she was worthless.

I wondered if the photographers who took these kinds of pictures ever thought about what they were doing. Did they even care about these girls? Then an awful thought came to me. "Mom," I asked, "does somebody make girls do this?"

"Sometimes," she said. "But some girls do it willingly because they want the money. Some of them don't see anything wrong with it. Isn't that sad?"

"Yeah," I whispered. Then I told her, "I really am sorry. I found this stuff by accident, and once I got started . . . well . . . it was just so tempting. But I won't look at it anymore. I promise."

"Pornography can be more than just a temptation, Ryan," said Mom. "It can actually become addictive, like alcohol or drugs. A lot of people even need counseling to deal with it." She put an arm around me. "So I'm going to help you with this problem, OK?"

I thought about all the times I couldn't resist looking at porn. I didn't think I was addicted, but I *was* afraid I'd have trouble keeping my promise. "OK," I said. "Thanks."

I'm not thrilled that Mom's "helping" me by getting rid of our data plan and moving the computer to the living room where she can watch me like a hawk. But I know she has to do that stuff. How else am I going to get past this problem?

I'm a little worried about that. To tell you the truth, I can see myself doing it all again if the opportunity presents itself. But I have a plan for that situation. First, I'll remind myself those girls are real people who deserve some respect. Then, I'll say a prayer for them and ask God to help them make their lives better. And I'll pray for myself, too. *Give me strength, Lord!*

And until I'm in control, I'm planning to use the computer less and live real life more. Maybe I'll even leave the house once in a while and I don't know . . . talk to a friend? Get some exercise? Or, hey, spend more time out there actually taking photographs!

DISCUSSION QUESTIONS

1. The Church teaches us to respect the human body. How does pornography contradict that teaching?

2. Some people claim pornography is "victimless," but that isn't really true. How does pornography hurt the people involved in making it? How does it hurt the people who view it?

3. In what ways could pornography affect your relationships with others? In what ways could it affect your relationship with Jesus?

4. What do you think a person should do if he or she accidentally discovers pornography online?

5. When someone is tempted to keep viewing pornography, how can he or she resist? How could you help that person live his or her faith in Jesus?

ACTIVITY

Write a letter to Ryan about his experiences. Encourage him and give him suggestions about resisting temptation.

PRAYER

Lord, sometimes I am tempted by images I see online
or in other media. It's so easy to think only of myself as I view
the bodies of other people and use what I see for my own
pleasure or entertainment.
Give me the strength to turn away from these temptations,
to ask for help when I need it,
and to always respect not just the human body,
but the whole human person. Amen.

THE MESSAGE

Even though you know looking at pornographic images conflicts with Christian values, you may still find them tempting. The good news is that temptation is not the same as sin. Remember, too, that even if we do fall, God still loves us. He will always forgive us and give us the strength we need to try again. To fight the temptation of pornography, try some of the suggestions below:

- Control the computer itself. Move the computer to an area where it's easily visible, and install filtering software. (Adults can help with this.) Limit time online to what's needed for homework and necessary communication.

- Keep active. Resistance is harder when you're feeling stressed. Release tension with physical activities like playing sports, taking a walk, doing yard work, or even cleaning your room.

- Spend time in the real world. Avoid being alone. Do things with your family, get together with friends, participate in church and school activities, and become involved in service.

- Turn to God. He will give you the strength you need. Pray to him often and specifically about whatever you find tempting. Try reading his word daily. Go to Mass more often and receive the sacraments frequently.

- Internet Pornography
- Cyberbullying
- Modesty
- Family
- Materialism
- Dishonesty
- Body Image
- Success
- Depression
- Substance Abuse

CYBERBULLYING

THE ISSUE

THE FACTS

Cyberbullying is harassing, teasing, threatening, or embarrassing someone using communications technology like the Internet or cell phones. Unlike "old-fashioned" bullying, which is limited to times the bully is present, cyberbullying can occur around the clock. One-third to one-half of teens have been bullied online, and just as many teens engage in cyberbullying others. Common bullying activities include sending harassing or threatening texts, emails, and instant messages; stealing passwords to lock others out of their accounts; distributing private photos; impersonating others in order to embarrass them or damage friendships; teasing and insulting others on blogs, websites, and social network pages; and many more hurtful actions. Cyberbullies often view their behavior as inconsequential, fun, or even well-deserved. However, cyberbullying can be devastating to the victims, causing self-esteem issues, trouble in school, absenteeism, depression, relationship problems, drug and alcohol abuse, and even suicide.

SCRIPTURE

A perverse person spreads strife, and a whisperer separates close friends.

Proverbs 16:28

Let no evil talk come out of your mouths, but only what is useful for building up, as there is need, so that your words may give grace to those who hear.

Ephesians 4:29

CATECHISM

Respect for the reputation of persons forbids every attitude and word likely to cause them unjust injury. He becomes guilty:
—of *rash judgment* who, even tacitly, assumes as true, without sufficient foundation, the moral fault of a neighbor;
—of *detraction* who, without objectively valid reason, discloses another's faults and failings to persons who did not know them;
—of *calumny* who, by remarks contrary to the truth, harms the reputation of others and gives occasion for false judgments concerning them.

CCC no. 2477

Trumors

OK, I admit it: I love those juicy celebrity gossip sites. They're shallow, I know, but fun, too. So much fun that I decided to start a gossip site for my own school, Truman Central. I called it "Trumors" which worked as a mashup of "Truman" and "rumors" but could also mean "true rumors." How perfect was that?

At first I planned to post as "Di-on-the-Wall," but then I realized I could dig up more dirt anonymously. So I created a fake network personality called "Shehunose," friended everyone I could, and waited for people to find their way to Trumors where I'd already posted:

Rah, rah! Cheerie dearie chats up Mr. Adorkable. Shehunose sez luv is in the air.

Yep, Macho the Jock hits the dance studio twice a week. Y hide it, bro?

Sweet teach gets engaged! Shehunose sez congrats and OOH-LA-LA!

The next morning, I had thirty comments. And when I got to school, lots of people were buzzing about Trumors—including my friends.

"It's nice Mademoiselle O'Hara is getting married," Jessie was saying.

"That was news," said Elena. "But I already knew Amber liked that brainiac Harrison."

"You know, he really *is* cute," said Lily like the idea just occurred to her. In reality, she'd already expressed that opinion to at least a dozen people.

My friends would be impressed to know I was behind the gossip, but I just said I'd found the site, too, and asked, "Who do you think the dancing guy is?"

I posted fresh dirt every evening after that, always sticking close to the truth to build a good reputation as Shehunose. Soon everybody in school was following and talking about Trumors. I was the Queen of Gossip!

I was feeling pretty great, until the day Lily embarrassed me in PE. We had to run laps, and I came in dead last. No big deal. But then Lily said, "See, Di? You were so wrong. Catching athlete's foot *doesn't* make you any better at sports."

I smiled as everyone laughed at her lame joke, but I was mortified. Now people thought I had nasty feet. And Lily acted like she didn't even know she'd embarrassed me. If she could only experience what I was feeling . . .

But she could—thanks to Shehunose. That night I posted:

Hey, Mr. Adorkable. Flower girl wants U 4 herself. Watch out, Cheerie!

When I got to school the next day, Jessie and Elena were talking about my latest post.

"How does she know this stuff?" said Jessie. "She really is 'She who knows'!"

"Oh, lots of people already knew Lily liked Harrison," said Elena.

"But Harrison didn't," said Jessie. "Lily must be so embarrassed."

"Yeah," I said as seriously as I could.

Jessie frowned. "That Shehunose is kind of mean."

"Come on," I said. "It's just a little gossip."

When Lily arrived, she complained, "I can't

believe there's a trumor about me. How humiliating!" But she smiled as she told us about Harrison talking to her on the bus.

The whole thing could have ended right there. But when people called me "Toad Toes" and "The Fungus" all day, Lily never once admitted her remark was just a joke. It was only fair for her to be embarrassed, too. That night I posted:

Mr. A and FG make luv connection. Shehunose sez ain't they cute? FG sez he's all mine!

"I never said that!" Lily told us the next morning. "But at least Harrison didn't believe it. He's not mad at all."

Elena pointed down the hall. "Somebody is."

Amber stomped our way, tossed a dirty name at Lily, and walked on.

"She hates me now," said Lily. "And it's all because of . . . of . . . Shehu-*lies*!"

"Everything on Trumors is true!" I cried.

"But I didn't say what she said I said," Lily said.

I rolled my eyes. "That part's a joke."

But she insisted Shehunose had lied, and the others agreed. Then they started talking about whether Amber would stay mad. I was too steamed about Lily's slam to listen closely.

"Yoohoo!" Elena waved a hand in my face. "We're going to class now, Di."

"Yeah, move those hobbit feet," said Lily.

I just did not believe that girl! She couldn't handle it when somebody got real about her, but it was OK if she spread humiliating lies. And now she was calling me names? So far Shehunose had gone pretty easy on Lily, but it was time to really get back at her.

Over the next week, I included several embarrassing posts about Lily among my other trumors. Of course, I kept it all real, but sometimes I exaggerated just for laughs. Like when Harrison and Lily sat together at lunch, I wrote it up as a romantic date. And after Lily pulled a drier sheet out of her shirt in the locker room, I joked about Flower Girl stuffing her bra.

"That Shehunose is nothing but a bully," said Jessie one morning.

"How is it bullying when what she writes is true?" I demanded.

Lily pouted. "But people are making fun of me. I hate it!"

Now she knew how I felt! Thanks to her, people still teased me about my feet. Embarrassing her back might seem like bullying to my friends, but I called it justice.

Since Harrison was so nice about the trumors, Lily liked him more than ever. She hung around all the time just adoring him. I *had* to post about that:

Arf barf! Shehunose sez stop following Mr. A around like a puppy dog, FG. Drooling is pathetic!

"It's cyberbullying," Elena said the next morning.

"Definitely," said Jessie. "She's gone too far."

I started to ask why they didn't stop reading Trumors if they felt like that, but Lily arrived just then. Her eyes were so puffy you could tell she'd been crying—probably for hours. "Everyone's talking about me," she whispered with trembling lips.

The other girls hugged her and said supportive stuff, but I just stood there, frozen. I never thought she'd get that upset. It wasn't my fault Lily was sensitive, was it? So I embarrassed her a little! Besides, she did exactly the same thing to me.

Well, maybe not *exactly.* Lily had dropped her joke a while ago and I was still going after her. That was different. And what she did wasn't about revenge. I didn't think she set out to hurt me, but I actually *tried* to make her feel bad.

Wait. That *is* how bullies act. My heart fell to the floor as I realized my friends were right. Shehunose really was a cyberbully, and Shehunose was me!

All day long and into the evening, I thought about that and tried to figure out a way to fix things. But it's just impossible to unhurt anybody. Finally, I prayed for God's help, and that's when I realized what I had to do.

I sat down then and wrote my last post for Trumors. After I admitted to spreading lies, I announced I was closing down the site. I ended the post with:

I'm sorry.

Those two words were the most important part of my message. This final post was my only chance to apologize to Lily—and anybody else I might have hurt—because I didn't have the guts to reveal my identity.

My heart seemed a little lighter after I finished, but I knew things wouldn't really be over and done until I received God's forgiveness. Luckily I didn't have to wait for Reconciliation to start acting like the person I wanted to be. I could become Shehu-*cares* right now.

DISCUSSION QUESTIONS

1. Bullying takes many forms, and is done for many reasons. What do you think causes someone to become a bully?

2. In what ways is cyberbullying more difficult for the victim than "regular" bullying? What are the best ways to stand up to bullying?

3. Tell about a time you observed cyberbullying. What did you do? What should you have done?

4. Is it OK to gossip as long as you stick to "true rumors"? Why or why not?

5. It's tempting to use our modern technology to intimidate or get back at others. What does Jesus teach about revenge? How can you follow his teachings and help others to do so?

ACTIVITY

For one week, use the Internet to make others feel good about themselves. Write a paragraph, poem, song, or story about your experience.

PRAYER

Lord, it's easy to abuse the power of today's communication technology.
Give me the wisdom to use it responsibly,
and help me carry out my virtual interactions
with the same kindness and respect
you want me to bring to all my relationships. Amen.

THE MESSAGE

Since cyberbullying doesn't involve close contact or physical force, it's not as easy to recognize that you're doing it. You may feel your online activities are harmless or funny, and never realize you're hurting somebody. How do you know if you've crossed the line? If you can answer yes to any of the following questions, you may be engaging in cyberbullying:

- Have you ever texted or posted rude comments or insults to or about anyone?

- Have you used your online presence to get back at people?

- Have you flagged posts that didn't deserve it or started warning wars?

- Have you ever forwarded photos, emails, texts, or anything else someone wanted to keep private?

- Have you spread rumors or lies online?

- Have you posted Internet poll questions that are likely to encourage insulting responses?

- Have you impersonated others so you can do embarrassing things in their name?

- Have you ever threatened someone online—even as a joke?

- Do you keep your identity secret so you don't have to worry about the consequences of your online behavior?

- Have you ever posted something negative tonline that you would never say in person?

MODESTY

THE ISSUE

Internet Pornography
Cyberbullying
Modesty
Family
Materialism
Dishonesty
Body Image
Success
Depression
Substance Abuse

Chapter 3

THE FACTS

Fashions come and go, but modesty always seems to be an issue for teens. Today's young people are bombarded with media images that glorify sexiness and make displaying the body seem normal. Many teens feel pressured to wear immodest styles in order to fit in. Even if they wish to dress appropriately, finding modest but attractive clothing can prove difficult. Though modesty applies to boys as well as girls, females face more wardrobe choices and greater expectations to present themselves as sexually attractive. When male teens are surveyed about immodest dress in girls, they admit to lustful thoughts. While most accept responsibility for those reactions, many appreciate it when a girl dresses modestly because it helps them focus on making a genuinely personal connection with her.

SCRIPTURE

Lead us not into temptation, but deliver us from evil.

Matthew 6:13

Do you not know that you are God's temple and that God's Spirit dwells in you?

1 Corinthians 3:16

CATECHISM

Purity requires *modesty*, an integral part of temperance. Modesty protects the intimate center of the person. It means refusing to unveil what should remain hidden. It is ordered to chastity to whose sensitivity it bears witness. It guides how one looks at others and behaves toward them in conformity with the dignity of persons and their solidarity.

CCC no. 2521

Modesty protects the mystery of persons and their love. It encourages patience and moderation in loving relationships; it requires that the conditions for the definitive giving and commitment of man and woman to one another be fulfilled. Modesty is decency. It inspires one's choice of clothing. It keeps silence or reserve where there is evident risk of unhealthy curiosity. It is discreet.

CCC no. 2522

My Body Is a Temple!

I hate to admit this, but I used to be a slug. I moved as little as possible and consumed tons of junk food and gallons of soda. Of course, I was in terrible condition. After a shopping trip last spring tired me out, I decided to take action. All summer long, I ate healthier foods and exercised regularly. By the start of school, I was in the best shape of my life.

"The guys are checking you out, Sofi," my best friend, Angel, told me our first day back.

"They are?" Boys never paid attention to me!

"Definitely," she said. "Hey, you should get some new outfits to go with your new body. Then they'll really notice you."

After school, we hit our favorite thrift shop where Angel talked me into trying on some tight, sexy jeans. When I came out of the dressing room, she went, "Whoa." I turned to the three-way mirror and found that I looked . . . well . . . amazing! Who knew I had the potential to be hot?

"It's time you had a whole new look," said Angel. "I'll help, OK?" She kept bringing me stuff to try on, and I ended up buying some slinky tops, two pairs of hot jeans, and a sassy skirt. (It was a good thing I wasn't paying full price!)

My new style was a big hit at school. As I walked down the halls each day, boys I hardly knew said hi. And guys starting sitting near me and talking to me. Too bad I wasn't allowed to date yet! I would have had plans every Saturday!

Actually, I wasn't even allowed to dress that way, but I managed to get away with it for a good while through the strategic use of hoodies and sweats. ("The air conditioning is freezing cold at school, Dad.") Then one day Mom walked into my bedroom just after I covered up. Two seconds earlier, and I would have been busted! That's when I started taking my sexy clothes to school and changing there.

All the male attention turned out to be a positive influence. Before my makeover, I never understood what it meant when someone said, "My body is my temple." Now I got it. If I wanted guys to admire my body, I had to make it worthy of their worship. And since an amazing body required a healthy lifestyle, I was really motivated to keep working on myself.

And to shop! I went to the thrift shops often—and to the mall now and then—and bought more attention-getting outfits. I had to dip into the cash I was saving for camp next summer—and sneak the stuff past my parents!—but it was definitely worth it. One day, I even had two guys arguing over who would get me a book off a high library shelf. They scuffled a bit, and the librarian made them sit down.

"Aren't they sweet?" I said to Angel, who was waiting nearby.

She snorted. "They're trying to look down your shirt. Not that you're making it much of a challenge."

She made me sound terrible! The library wasn't a good place to talk so I waited until we were out in the hall to set her straight. "There's nothing wrong with looking your best," I said, "and that's all I'm doing. I eat right. I exercise. I mean . . . my body is my temple. If guys want—"

"*Your* temple?" Angel interrupted. "It's supposed to be God's temple . . . a home for the Holy Spirit."

"Um . . . excuse me," I said. "Wasn't this whole makeover your idea?"

"Yeah, but I didn't mean for you to take it so far. You're just . . . it's like . . . oh, never mind. Let's get back to study hall."

I told myself Angel was dead wrong. My style was just more up-to-date and edgy than it used to be. So what? But all afternoon, I noticed that guys were giving me a whole-body once-over with their eyes.

That night I took a hard look at my new wardrobe. If my body was supposed to be God's temple, shouldn't I be treating it like something special instead of letting just any guy drool over it? I held up my flimsiest top and sighed. I had to admit I wasn't really comfortable when I wore stuff like that.

And what if my parents found out what I was doing? I was responsible for my own laundry, but Mom could decide to be nice and throw in a load for me. Looking in my hamper might give her a heart attack! From now on, I decided, I would dress more modestly!

So I started wearing cute-but-not-revealing outfits. Angel always said I looked nice, but other people kept asking embarrassing questions. Was I was going to a funeral? Did I need to do laundry? Had my grandma started dressing me? And the guys began to ignore me again!

One morning I just couldn't take it anymore. I put on a skimpy top, a thong, and my tightest jeans. When I looked in the mirror, I almost changed my mind. Those jeans hugged my body like a second skin, and the top was really revealing. But I pushed away my doubts, threw on an oversized sweatshirt, and hurried out, calling a good-bye to my parents as I left.

At school, lots of guys smiled at me (once I ditched the sweatshirt), but Angel frowned. "Sheesh, Sofi! Are you even wearing underwear?"

"Yes! Not that it's any of your business."

She folded her arms. "You're kind of making it the whole world's business. I thought you were going to respect your body and quit dressing like that."

"Hey, Sofi!" Brian from my first period class appeared at my elbow. "You look amazing."

"Thanks," I said. After talking to him a few minutes, I realized Angel was gone.

All day long, guys swarmed me, but Angel stayed away. She didn't even sit with me at lunch, but I had plenty of company without her. If she couldn't handle my new popularity, that was just too bad. I assumed we'd always support each other, but maybe Angel wasn't the friend I thought she was.

Later that day, I heard somebody saying my name behind a divider in the computer lab so I leaned closer to listen. When I realized some guys were making rude remarks about every part of my body, I ran out and hid in the bathroom to cry. I guess Angel followed me because soon she came in and asked, "What's wrong, Sofi?"

I explained what I'd heard. "They don't respect me as a person at all" I cried. Then I blew my nose and admitted the truth. "I guess it's not like *I've* been respecting myself either."

"No, you haven't," agreed Angel, but she said it kindly.

"I don't want to dress like this." I tried to pull my top into a less-revealing position, but there just wasn't enough material. "But I really want people to pay attention to me."

"Maybe you need some help," she said.

"It's not like there's rehab for that," I said sarcastically.

"No, but prayer can help. And so can I. I'll come over before school tomorrow."

Let me tell you—it was hard to give up my sexy

style. For a long time, I prayed every night about wanting guys to notice me, and let Angel choose my clothes every morning. (She can really put together an outfit that's cute *and* appropriate.) Finally I was able to dress myself again.

I feel like I have things under control now, but I haven't stopped praying. Even though some guys still like to talk to me (surprise! surprise!), I miss the attention I used to get. So I keep asking the Lord to help me stay on the right track. I really want people to respect me as a person. But I guess that has to start with me. My body truly *is* amazing!

I mean . . . because it's a gift from God.

DISCUSSION QUESTIONS

1. Inner character is much more important than outer appearance, but the way we dress communicates something to others. What do you want your style to say about you?

2. How does dressing modestly show respect to yourself? To others? To God?

3. Modesty doesn't apply just to girls. In what ways can boys be immodest?

4. How much influence do magazines, television, movies, and other media have on the current styles? How much influence do they have on you?

5. Besides dressing appropriately, how else can you treat your body as a temple of God?

ACTIVITY

Make a collage of images and/or words that communicate modesty and respect for the human body. Be ready to talk about why you chose the items in your collage.

PRAYER

Lord God, I'm so thankful for the body you gave me,
and I want to honor you by always respecting the person I am,
both inside and out.
Help me treat my body as the sacred and precious gift that it is.
Show me how to be modest in my dress and in my heart
so I can always be a living temple
for your Holy Spirit. Amen.

THE MESSAGE

You may think dressing modestly limits your ability to express your personality, but it can actually have the opposite effect. Modest clothing gives you the freedom to simply be yourself because the focus is on the *whole you* not just your body. So how do you decide what's appropriate to wear? Consider these guidelines:

- Think about where you're going and what you're doing. Clothing that's OK for playing sports or lounging at home may be inappropriate for a more formal occasion or place.

- Don't assume that dressing up means dressing sexy.

- Be sure you can move easily and sit comfortably in an outfit without revealing private body parts or intimate clothing.

- When you have to struggle to get into an item of clothing or do something deceptive to be able to wear it, think twice. It may not be appropriate!

- Ask yourself if your outfit highlights particular body parts in a way that could be distracting to others.

- Avoid clothing with images or messages that others might find offensive.

- If you wonder whether something you're wearing is over the line, it probably is. Pray about it, and ask God to help you decide for sure.

FAMILY

THE ISSUE

Internet Pornography

Cyberbullying

Modesty

Family

Materialism

Dishonesty

Body Image

Success

Depression

Substance Abuse

THE FACTS

As teens become more self-reflective, they realize other people might be thinking about them, too. Often, they assume they are being watched and judged. It's not unusual for teens to be anxious about how they appear to others, feel self-conscious, or become embarrassed more often or more easily than younger children or adults do. Because they are absorbed in developing a personal identity separate from their families, teens are especially concerned that the actions of their parents and siblings might negatively affect their social status. For the seven million American kids who have siblings with disabilities, being embarrassed by a family member can be a major concern. However, like their peers, they usually become less sensitive as they mature and more able to cope with and accept their families as they are.

SCRIPTURE

The commandment we have from him is this: those who love God must love their brothers and sisters also.

1 John 4:21

"Truly I tell you, just as you did it to one of the least of these who are members of my family, you did it to me."

Matthew 25:40

CATECHISM

The relationships within the family bring an affinity of feelings, affections and interests, arising above all from the members' respect for one another. The family is a *privileged community* called to achieve a "sharing of thought and common deliberation by the spouses as well as their eager cooperation as parents in the children's upbringing."

CCC no. 2206

Filial respect promotes harmony in all of family life; it also concerns *relationships between brothers and sisters.* Respect toward parents fills the home with light and warmth. "Grandchildren are the crown of the aged" (Proverbs 17:6). "With all humility and meekness, with patience, [support] one another in charity" (Ephesians 4:2).

CCC no. 2219

Chapter 4

The Noah Factor

Sometimes it feels like I have the world's weirdest brother. Don't get me wrong. Noah and I are pretty close even though he's two years younger. And I understand that his attention disorder and learning disabilities make life difficult for him. But the way he acts can get really embarrassing!

People at our old school got used to Noah dashing around and blurting out stuff and laughing his guts out. And they mostly accepted him—and me, too. But not too long ago we had to start over at a new school where nobody knew Noah. I was afraid that once they did, I'd never fit in.

My parents worry enough already so I didn't mention anything to them. But I did talk to Noah. "Be on your best behavior," I ordered. "Don't run! And think before you speak, OK?" He just folded his arms and looked at the ceiling so I repeated, "OK?"

"I'm thinking before I speak, Jake," he said. "Just like you told me." Then he heehawed at his own joke until he was gasping for breath. I was doomed to be an outcast!

On our first morning, I took Noah to the office to meet up with his special teacher, then I went to find my locker. The new school was HUGE, with halls so crowded that no one even noticed me—the new kid. I figured they'd be lucky to spot somebody they *did* know.

That's when I got the idea. In this big school—and with our different schedules—I probably wouldn't see my brother at all. Nobody needed to know I even *had* a brother. At least not yet. I could

work on making some friends first and deal with the Noah factor later.

For a moment, I felt guilty about wanting to keep my own brother a secret. But then I realized he'd never know it was happening so what was the harm? And didn't I deserve to live as myself for once—not just as Noah's brother?

In homeroom, I met some guys named Derek and Tai. We had the same schedule so they helped me find my morning classes. It looked like everything was off to a good start.

But while I was waiting in the lunch line with those guys, I heard something that made my heart drop. It was Noah's loud voice saying, "Where's my money?" over and over. He was at the end of the line, digging through his pockets. It wasn't even his lunch period!

I leaned back so he wouldn't spot me and do something embarrassing. Why should my social life be damaged by my strange brother? When I risked a peek, Noah had finally found his money and his teacher was leading him away. He waved at me, but I casually turned around as if I hadn't seen him.

Tai was staring straight at me. "Bizarre, huh?"

"Um . . . what?" I said, hoping he hadn't noticed anything.

"Broccoli on pizza," said Derek.

"Yeah," I said. "That's just not right."

The rest of the day went smoothly. When school let out, I avoided being seen with Noah by waiting inside until he got in our car. Then I dashed out and hopped in. As Mom drove off, I pointed out that it might be easier to pick us up at the side door where there was less traffic.

The next morning, I asked Dad to let us off at that same side door. When Noah and I got inside, I hurried toward my hall. Behind me I could hear my brother making race car noises as he zipped off toward his. Thank God nobody was around to see!

Things went really well that morning. I hung out with Tai and Derek and even talked to some other people. I was definitely starting to fit in.

Then Noah showed up while I was eating lunch! He ran in the cafeteria door, looking upset and darting his eyes all around. I just knew he was searching for me.

When his head was turned, I mumbled that I'd forgotten something, went back to the serving area, and stood behind the condiment bar until he left. Then I grabbed a package of something and returned to my table.

"What's the mayo for, Jake?" asked Tai.

Nothing on my tray took mayo so I said, "My fries. They're good like that." Then I had to actually eat them that way. Thanks to Noah.

After school, Mom made my life easier by coming to the side door like I'd suggested. The whole way home, Noah never mentioned whatever his problem was at lunch. If it wasn't important, then why did he have to make such a big deal over it?

I had a few more close calls with Noah over the next couple of days. Like having to duck into the science lab so I wouldn't pass him in the hall. And staying behind a shelf until he left the library. But mostly it was like he didn't even exist. It's not like I would ever want that for real! I was just doing what I needed to do to avoid his negative effects on my social life.

I knew my plan was working the day Derek said, "Hey, Jake. Tomorrow there's a game night in the gym. Why don't you come with us?"

"Yeah," said Tai.

"We'll go to my house after school," said Derek.

"My dad can drive us back later. OK?"

"Sure," I said. "Sounds good."

At game night lots of people talked to me. Things were going great—until my family showed up. I didn't mind so much that Mom and Dad came, but did they have to bring Noah along to ruin everything?

He saw me, and they all started waving. That's when I went into survival mode. It sounds really cold, but I acted like I didn't even know them. I mean . . . I looked right through them and then went back to my game.

As I turned away, I caught the hurt looks on my parents' faces, and I felt terrible. But I told myself it was mostly my brother's fault. If he just acted like he was normal, he wouldn't even *be* a factor in my social life. I wouldn't have to protect myself.

After the game was finished, I headed for the concession stand, but Noah stopped me in the hall. "I know you don't want me around," he said.

"I do, too!" I cried.

He folded his arms. "Right. That's why you keep hiding."

I was surprised he even realized what was going on! "It's not like that," I muttered.

"It's OK," he said with a sigh. "I get it. I'm embarrassing. But you shouldn't be mean to Mom and Dad because of me. I'll do something on the other side of the gym so you can talk to them, OK?" He walked off without waiting for an answer.

Lately I'd worried so much about my brother embarrassing me that I forgot about his good side. Nobody has a bigger heart than Noah! You can crush it flat—like I did—and he'll still have room inside to care about other people. Who *wouldn't* be proud to have a brother like that?

And how could I ever have blamed Noah for my behavior? I was ashamed of how I acted tonight—and every day since we started school here. I was a complete jerk—to my own family! And for what? Hurting them wasn't worth it even if I'd made a million friends.

For a good while, I stood in the hall, praying for God's help to fix the mess I'd made. Finally I gathered up the courage to go back in the gym and try to fix things with my family. I decided I'd start out by apologizing. That wouldn't be easy, but it was the first step in making things right.

And after that? Well, it was about time I started acting like someone who deserved to be Noah's brother. So I was going to introduce him to Tai and Derek and my other new friends. Maybe they'd accept him. Maybe they wouldn't. But from now on, everybody would know that Noah was a factor in my life.

DISCUSSION QUESTIONS

1. Think about a time when a family member embarrassed you. How did you react? How do you feel about the incident now?

2. Think about a time when *you* embarrassed someone else. How do you think that person felt? How did the incident affect your relationship?

3. Our faith teaches us to love all our brothers and sisters worldwide, but sometimes it seems hardest to be kind to the ones in our "real" family. Why do you think we tend to treat them less lovingly than we do other people?

4. When someone embarrasses you, does it matter if he or she meant to do so? Why or why not?

5. What are some good ways to cope with embarrassing situations?

6. How can you help someone who's embarrassed by serious family problems that can't be easily solved?

ACTIVITY

For two weeks, keep a gratitude journal about your family. Each day write something good about your family in general or about a particular family member. For your last entry, write a paragraph describing how you feel about your family.

PRAYER

Lord God, my family is not perfect, but neither am I. Give us the understanding we need to accept each other the way you made us, and the grace to forgive each other's flaws. Help us love and support each other even in embarrassing situations, and keep our family strong so that we may serve you. Amen.

THE MESSAGE

Nobody can embarrass you more than your own family! Fortunately, you can't actually die of embarrassment. (It only *feels* that way.) And you can improve the situation by remembering a few important facts:

- Your family members probably don't mean to hurt or embarrass you. They just don't realize how they're affecting you.

- If you can laugh about something embarrassing your family did, other people may not take it seriously either.

- And maybe it's not that bad anyway. Compare whatever happens to something truly tragic, and get some perspective.

- Sometimes you embarrass your family. You know it's true.

- You're part of a family, but you're a completely separate person, too. You're only responsible for your own actions.

- It's OK to talk to your family about their embarrassing behavior if you do it in a calm, respectful way. Don't attack! Just pick one thing and ask them to stop. But be ready for them to ask *you* to stop doing something too!

- Your family is a gift from God—and they're nonreturnable. So try to appreciate them for who they are and forgive them when they do something wrong. Remember, it isn't a sin to annoy or embarrass someone unintentionally!

Internet Pornography

• Cyber-bullying

~~Modesty~~

MATERIALISM

THE ISSUE

~~Family~~

• Materialism

• Dishonesty

• Body Image

• Success

• Depression

• Substance Abuse

Today's teens spend billions of dollars a year on clothing, video games, accessories, and other objects they want. While there's nothing wrong with owning and enjoying things, many young people (and adults, too) overvalue possessions. Studies show that teens often define success and self-esteem in terms of what they have. When surveyed, over two-thirds of teens claim they would be happier if they could spend more money on themselves, and many say they would rather spend their time buying things than doing any other activity. Unfortunately, research consistently shows that materialistic people are less happy than others and not as satisfied with their lives.

SCRIPTURE

And he said to them, "Take care! Be on your guard against all kinds of greed; for one's life does not consist in the abundance of possessions."

Luke 12:15

"Do not store up for yourselves treasures on earth, where moth and rust consume and where thieves break in and steal; but store up for yourselves treasures in heaven, where neither moth nor rust consumes and where thieves do not break in and steal. For where your treasure is, there your heart will be also."

Matthew 6:19–21

CATECHISM

Jesus enjoins his disciples to prefer him to everything and everyone, and bids them "renounce all that [they have]" for his sake and that of the Gospel. Shortly before his passion he gave them the example of the poor widow of Jerusalem who, out of her poverty, gave all that she had to live on. The precept of detachment from riches is obligatory for entrance into the Kingdom of heaven.

CCC no. 2544

All Christ's faithful are to "direct their affections rightly, lest they be hindered in their pursuit of perfect charity by the use of worldly things and by an adherence to riches which is contrary to the spirit of evangelical poverty."

CCC no. 2545

Chapter 5

The Collector

Legendary.

That's the only way to describe my video game collection. I have every single game that's available for my system. My friends love coming to my house, of course!

Not that collecting games is an earth-shaking achievement. But everyone needs to be proud of something, right? And I can honestly say my collection is pretty darn impressive.

Which is why I couldn't understand Adam's behavior the first time he came over. We had both joined our school's new service club, and I invited him home one afternoon. When we walked into the family room, he actually said, "So what do you want to do, Colin?" Like he wasn't surrounded by video games!

"Gee, I don't know. Play a game?" I gestured toward my vast collection.

"Oh. OK." He pulled Motoburst, an auto racing game, from a shelf. "How about this one?"

"An oldie but a goodie." I set things up, and we traded wins until he had to go. Then I said, "We'll try something else next time." I motioned toward the crowded shelves again, expecting some kind of reaction.

But Adam just said, "OK. Thanks. See you at school." Then he left!

I didn't get it. Adam wasn't very impressed by my epic collection. I figured he was one of those low-key guys who doesn't show much enthusiasm.

But at the next service club meeting, Adam got plenty excited talking about the family shelter.

"They give homeless families a place to live," he told us, "and provide job training for the parents and school for the kids and . . ." He got more and more worked up as he went on. At the end, he practically shouted "We should help!"

Everybody agreed—including me. Our faculty advisor offered to contact the shelter and ask what we could do. At the next meeting we made plans to volunteer at the shelter one afternoon a week, starting next week.

I was surprised Adam could get that stoked about anything, but I didn't know him very well. At least not yet. After the meeting, I invited him to come over that weekend. "Some friends will be there," I told him. "And we can play video games."

"Sounds great," he said.

On Saturday, my friends Lucas and Raj were friendly to Adam even though he'd never been part of our group. Everybody talked some, then Lucas asked me, "Did you get Yestermaze?"

I whipped that game off the shelf. "Here it is!"

"He always has the newest releases," Raj told Adam.

"Cool," said Adam like he was talking about the weather.

"But wait—there's more!" I cried, showing them the latest dragon-slaying game, too.

"Whoa! Can you believe it?" Lucas asked Adam.

"Um . . . no," he replied.

Adam's attitude really bugged me. He just didn't seem to care about what I had to offer. I worked hard on my collection, and nobody around could beat it. Everybody else respected that—Adam hardly even noticed!

Still, he seemed like a nice enough guy—especially when we went to the family shelter. He was great with the little kids there, taking them outside and teaching them old games like Freeze Tag and Simon Says. I helped him, but he ran everything.

Later, while other club members helped to serve dinner, Adam and I washed pots and pans. I was happy to be helping out, so I decided to give him some credit. "Volunteering here is a fantastic idea," I said.

"Thanks," he replied. "Seeing these kids makes you appreciate what you have, doesn't it?"

"It sure does," I said. And I meant that! Next to the homeless kids, I felt lucky to have a house and plenty of food and lots of stuff. That night, I said a prayer for them.

But after that, I didn't think about the kids much. And by the time the weekend rolled around—and the guys came over again—I wasn't feeling fortunate any more.

"Before you even ask," I told Lucas, Raj, and Adam, "I did not get Warrior Piglets."

"You didn't?" cried Raj.

"No! I don't have any more money saved, and my parents wouldn't buy it. They said the new releases are coming out too fast now for me to get them all." I flopped onto the couch with a sigh.

"You have plenty of other games," said Adam.

He just did not get it! "It's a *collection*," I told him. "And now it's not complete."

"That's OK, Colin," said Raj.

"Yeah," said Lucas. "We can find something else to play today. Right, Adam?"

"Of course!" he said. "There's only every game on the planet here."

"Not Warrior Piglets," I muttered.

We all had a good time that afternoon, but I was still annoyed about the missing game. It wasn't the end of the world, but who wants to be the guy with *most* of a collection? That doesn't make you anybody special.

Just before leaving, Adam said, "You don't have to have everything, you know. They're just games."

"I know that!" I cried. "But they're my thing, OK? They're part of who I am."

He shook his head, but all he said was, "See you later."

I had really had it with him. My collection meant a lot to me, sure, but I knew we were just talking about games, OK? I didn't need some lecture from Adam!

The next time the service club volunteered at the shelter, I agreed to help Adam again even though I was tired of him.

Since it was rainy, Adam led us all to a game room that had a ping pong table, some board games, and a small TV with—yes!—a gaming platform like mine. "I'll help with this," I told Adam, turning on the system.

A few kids hurried over. Motoburst was already plugged in so I passed out the controllers and let them play that awhile. After a bit, I popped out the game and said, "Want to try something else?"

"That's the only game we have," said one little boy.

"But it's the most fun," said somebody else.

"Yeah," I said. "It . . . it sure is." I put the game back in and they played some more while I sat there feeling funny.

"Play with me, Adam!" one of the girls called.

"You're dead meat!" Adam joked, grabbing a controller. He made the game more fun by kidding around, but he couldn't change the sad fact that it was the only one there.

Looking around, I noticed other problems, too. The ping pong table didn't have a net. And the board games must have belonged to King Tut's grandpa. How could I ever have complained about not being able to get Warrior Piglets? It was embarrassing to realize how good I had it—and how little I'd appreciated that!

The girl zoomed her car over the finish line first, and Adam made everybody laugh by whining, "You always beat me!"

That's when I understood that he must have been volunteering here for some time. No wonder he wasn't impressed with me and my games! He was more interested in helping other people than being somebody with . . . well . . . somebody with a bunch of cool stuff.

And who was I *without* that stuff? To tell you the truth, I wasn't sure, but I did have some idea about who I wanted to be. And it wasn't a guy who cared more about things than people.

I wish I could say I donated all my games to the shelter after that, but I'm only human, and I love my stuff. I did set aside a pretty big stack for the kids at the shelter, though. Maybe I'll be able to give them a few more things later. In the meantime, I'm going to help out as much as I can. I figure it's time I had a new game plan for my life.

Discussion Questions

1. How do we know Jesus did not place a high value on possessions? What can we do to follow his teachings?

2. Have you ever bought or received something you really wanted, and then been disappointed by it in some way? What was it, and why were you disappointed?

3. Possessions don't give lasting satisfaction or make our lives meaningful. What does?

4. What's the difference between needing something and just wanting it? Name some things that fit each category.

5. In what ways does our culture pressure us to desire things? How can our faith help us resist that pressure?

6. What are your favorite possessions? What would your life be like without them?

Activity

Sort your personal possessions into categories like clothing, games, books, etc. Count each category, and display the information in a chart or graph. Select at least one item to donate to charity. Be ready to discuss your experience.

Prayer

Lord, help me keep my priorities straight,
putting faith and family, people and purpose,
before things. Give me the wisdom to focus on what
matters in life and the strength to control my desire
for possessions. Above all, open my heart to the
needs of others. Amen.

The Message

Our culture encourages materialism, but we don't have to buy into that! We can focus on what God teaches us to value instead of caring so much about possessions. How can you live in our society and resist the power of stuff? Try these suggestions:

- Give before you get. Before you buy something for yourself, donate to your church or a charity.

- Wait. If buying something is a good idea, holding off a few weeks won't matter. You might feel less enthused about the purchase later.

- De-clutter. You may have multiples of the same accessory or several similar articles of clothing. Go through everything, and donate whatever you can.

- Keep things balanced. Once you've de-cluttered, plan to get rid of something old whenever you buy something new. That way you won't be overwhelmed by stuff again.

- Mute or skip TV ads. Commercials are designed to tempt you. Ignore them.

- Do something besides shop. Simple activities like talking, exercising, drawing, reading, and volunteering can be more fun and satisfying than you might think.

- Take time daily to thank God for the good things in your life. Gratitude for what you have decreases your desire for more.

Internet Pornography

Cyberbullying

Modesty

Family

DISHONESTY

THE ISSUE

Materialism

Dishonesty

Body Image

Success

Depression

Substance Abuse

THE FACTS

Though research shows that almost all teens believe dishonest actions like cheating, stealing, and lying are wrong, studies also reveal that almost all teens engage in these behaviors. Lying is a particular problem for kids. In surveys, 78–98 percent of teens admitted to lying to parents and teachers in the past year, usually to escape punishment or to test and expand their boundaries. Lying to friends is less acceptable to teens, but it's still common for them to do it in order to avoid conflict, get attention, or improve their social status. While almost all teens think honesty is important in relationships, they also feel that lying is often justified, and many even claim it's necessary for success in life. Despite the discrepancy between their beliefs and their behavior, most teens think of themselves as ethical.

SCRIPTURE

Lying lips are an abomination to the LORD, but those who act faithfully are his delight.

Proverbs 12:22

So then, putting away falsehood, let all of us speak the truth to our neighbors, for we are members of one another.

Ephesians 4:25

CATECHISM

By its very nature, lying is to be condemned. It is a profanation of speech, whereas the purpose of speech is to communicate known truth to others. The deliberate intention of leading a neighbor into error by saying things contrary to the truth constitutes a failure in justice and charity. The culpability is greater when the intention of deceiving entails the risk of deadly consequences for those who are led astray.

CCC no. 2485

Since it violates the virtue of truthfulness, a lie does real violence to another. It affects his ability to know, which is a condition of every judgment and decision. It contains the seed of discord and all consequent evils. Lying is destructive of society; it undermines trust among men and tears apart the fabric of social relationships.

CCC no. 2486

It's a Jungle Out There!

I'm not really into nature. Oh, I'm glad we have it, and I believe in taking care of the environment, I just don't enjoy roughing it in the great outdoors. For me AC, Internet, and TV are *not* optional. OK?

But when my friend Natalie begged me to go to camp with her this year, I couldn't say no. It's always so boring while she's away. And I figured I should try it once—for her.

I just didn't realize what camp would be like. (Besides . . . you know . . . outside.) When we arrived, the place was swarming with people I didn't know. But they all seemed to be friends with each other—and Natalie.

"This is Liz, my best friend from home," Natalie told everyone who talked to her.

And each one said, "Hi, Liz." Then ignored me.

It was terrible to feel like such an outsider! So I was really glad when a cute guy talked to me in the registration line. He glimpsed at my schedule and said, "So you're into canoeing?"

Since canoeing took place outdoors, the answer to his question was . . . that's right . . . no. But I wasn't about to admit I was only signing up because my friend did. Not when someone was finally speaking with me! "You bet," I said. "I love it." And maybe I would once I gave it a try.

"I put it on my schedule, too." He had reached the front of the line so he turned around to register. I tried to think of some clever remark to keep our conversation going, but my brain wasn't quick enough. He turned back and said, "Well . . . see you around." Then he headed toward the cabins.

Natalie and some other girls watched him until he was out of sight.

After I registered, I came and stood beside Natalie. One of the girls with her demanded, "Why was David Kingston talking to you?"

Everybody stared like they couldn't wait for my answer. The real conversation wouldn't impress anyone so I exaggerated things a bit. "He was interested in the activities I'm taking. Very interested. And he said he's hoping to see me again soon."

The other girls looked at me with respect, and the girl who questioned me said, "I'm Anya. What did you say your name was?"

We did introductions again, and I learned the other girls were Carlie, Juana, and Grace. We were all in the same cabin so we went there next to get settled in.

While we unpacked, the other girls caught up with each other and I was ignored again. Were they losing interest already? I'd never make it socially if that happened!

So when Carlie asked if anybody had a boyfriend, I smiled and said, "Maybe." Natalie's jaw dropped, and I quickly added, "But I never kiss and tell." Everyone laughed, and I shot a please-don't-rat-me-out look at Natalie. She didn't.

But on the way to the evening cookout, she pulled me aside. "Why did you lie?"

"I just said maybe!" She frowned so I explained, "I was trying to sound interesting, OK? And make some friends."

"Don't worry," she said. "It'll happen."

"If I can survive long enough out here in the wild," I joked. "I just saw a mosquito as big as a chicken!"

Natalie smiled. "That was a gnat. The mosquitoes look more like eagles."

At the cookout, we had to roast hot dogs over a fire like pioneers, but at least some people talked to me. At one point, Juana and Grace pumped me about my "boyfriend," but I kept acting mysterious. All I said was that he was nice. And we weren't exclusive. At least not yet. But who knew?

It looked like camp would be OK! I don't believe in actual lying, of course, but stretching the truth was no big deal. And it had really gotten me some acceptance.

Unfortunately, things started going wrong the next morning. David stopped by our table at breakfast and asked Natalie, "What have you been up to lately?" They talked a bit about the past year then he said, "See you all later."

Once he walked away, everybody looked at me. Anya said, "If he's so interested, why didn't he say anything to *you*?"

I guess camp was already honing my survival instincts because I thought fast. "Maybe he knows," I said. "About . . . about Jackson."

"So that's his name," said Grace. She turned to the others. "Her boyfriend."

Everybody went, "O-o-oh!" Except for Natalie, who knew Jackson was my chocolate lab.

When we left the mess hall together, she pounced. "That really was a lie, Liz."

"Not exactly! And they'll never find out anyway. Nobody here knows me—except you."

"I'm not so sure I want to," she muttered.

It was easy for her to say that. She already fit in here, but camp was a whole new frontier for me! I *couldn't* let people know I exaggerated David's interest. Then they might not believe the other things I said, and I'd be friendless again.

My first activity of the day was canoeing. (Hoo. Ray.) Anya and Juana were taking it at the same time as Natalie and me—and so was David! Would he out me when he discovered I knew absolutely nothing about boating?

Juana saw me looking his way. "He should know you're still available, Liz. I'm going to talk to him."

"Don't do that!" I cried.

"Did you decide you like Jackson better?" Anya asked.

"Maybe," I said. "He *is* really loyal."

Natalie rolled her eyes.

"But you like David, too, right?" said Juana.

"Sure." I wished they'd stop talking so I could think. My whole survival strategy was going to collapse if I didn't do something quick!

Only one idea sprang to mind so I went for it. "I don't feel so great," I said, trying to look woozy. I turned to Natalie. "It's that thing I have. You know."

"What thing?" she said.

I swayed a bit. "That . . . health . . . thing." When she shrugged, I snapped, "That thing where I faint!"

"Oh, that. Well, it looks like you're feeling better now." She walked off and started talking to David.

Like she couldn't play along with me one more time! Now the other girls looked suspicious, and I had to do something to save myself. "Natalie's supposed to be my friend," I said, "but look! She's trying to get David for herself."

My little distraction seemed to work. Anya and Juana watched Natalie and David a moment then started saying sympathetic stuff to me. Suddenly, I felt sick for real. "I need to go to the nurse's office," I said, running off.

The nurse had me rest on a cot. I turned toward the wall and fought off tears. I never should have come to camp! It was like a jungle, and not because of all the nature everywhere. Surviving socially was the real challenge, and I hadn't handled it very well. I got so desperate to impress people and get their attention. And all the excuses in the world couldn't change the truth. I lied—even about my best friend. Once she found out, our friendship would be over.

"Are you OK?"

I rolled over. Natalie was standing there. Just seeing the concern on her face made me burst into tears. I blubbered out the story of how I betrayed her then cried, "I'm so sorry! Can you ever forgive me?"

"I . . . I don't know," she said and then hurried out of the room.

I knew God would want me to come clean with everyone else, too, so I told my cabinmates the truth later. Of course, they made sure all the other campers knew what a liar I was. The rest of my time at camp was terrible. Oh, some people were really forgiving about the whole thing, but others gave me nothing but mean looks and cold shoulders.

Natalie was somewhere in-between. We weren't exactly friendly, but she didn't totally cut me off either. I worried about what our relationship would be like once we got home. Had my dishonesty ruined our friendship for good?

I figure I'm never going to camp again—even if they hold it inside! (There's something else I should have been honest about!) But that's not really important. Being the honest person God wants me to be—that's what matters. And working things out with the friends I have. Especially Natalie. Every day I pray our friendship will somehow survive.

Discussion Questions

1. What are some reasons people lie? Have you ever been in a situation that you felt justified lying?

2. Can someone be too honest? Explain your answer.

3. How do you feel when other people are dishonest with you? What effect has dishonesty had on your relationships?

4. How can a lie be harmful even if it is never discovered?

5. In what ways does our culture discourage honesty?

6. What does our faith teach us about honesty? How can we live out those teachings?

Activity

Make a list of situations in which someone might be tempted to lie to parents, friends, a teacher, or another person. Role-play each scenario twice, demonstrating both dishonest and honest behavior.

Prayer

It's hard to be honest, Lord,
so I sometimes let myself wander from the truth.
Keep me on the right track in my words and my actions,
and make me someone other people can trust.
Help me speak and live the truth. Amen.

The Message

Keeping it honest isn't easy, but it's an important part of living your faith. The first step in becoming a more honest person is being honest with yourself. Almost everyone *says* that dishonest behaviors are wrong, but they keep doing them anyway. Many people draw the line at certain actions like shoplifting or cheating but then give themselves a free pass to lie. Remember, honesty isn't just not telling lies. It also means telling the truth when you are asked to do so. How honest are you—really?

If you've committed any of the dishonest behaviors listed below, there's room for improvement:

- Told your parents you did something you didn't really do;
- Told your parents you didn't do something when you did;
- Given a teacher a false excuse;
- Let somebody else take the blame for something that was your fault;
- Used exaggeration to make yourself seem more impressive;
- Copied someone else's work—even with their permission;
- Kept something you found or received accidentally;
- Passed on a rumor you suspected was untrue;
- Made a promise you never intended to keep;
- Invented an excuse or story just to make it easier to deal with someone.

BODY IMAGE

THE ISSUE

- Internet Pornography
- Cyberbullying
- Modesty
- Family
- Materialism
- Dishonesty
- Body Image
- Success
- Depression
- Substance Abuse

THE FACTS

Since they're going through so many physical changes, teens tend to focus a lot of attention on their bodies. They compare themselves to their peers, to celebrities, and to the models in manipulated media images. Feeling they don't measure up, teens can become hypercritical of their appearances and develop negative body images. In studies, large numbers of teens—both girls and boys—report dissatisfaction with their bodies. For girls, body image is often negatively affected by early physical development or perceived weight problems. Boys tend to be more troubled by maturing late or being underweight as they feel great pressure to be muscular, strong, and manly-looking. For both sexes, negative body image can lead to poor self-esteem, depression, anxiety, and unhealthy efforts to achieve physical perfection.

SCRIPTURE

I praise you, for I am fearfully and wonderfully made. Wonderful are your works; that I know very well.

Psalm 139:14

[R]ather, let your adornment be the inner self with the lasting beauty of a gentle and quiet spirit, which is very precious in God's sight.

1 Peter 3:4

" . . . the LORD does not see as mortals see; they look on the outward appearance, but the LORD looks on the heart."

1 Samuel 16:7

CATECHISM

The human body shares in the dignity of "the image of God": it is a human body precisely because it is animated by a spiritual soul, and it is the whole human person that is intended to become, in the body of Christ, a temple of the Spirit:

> Man, though made of body and soul, is a unity. Through his very bodily condition he sums up in himself the elements of the material world. Through him they are thus brought to their highest perfection and can raise their voice in praise freely given to the Creator. For this reason man may not despise his bodily life. Rather he is obliged to regard his body as good and to hold it in honor since God has created it and will raise it up on the last day.

CCC no. 364

181 Ways to Get Out of PE

You know those big, buff guys you see on TV? The ones with broad shoulders and bulging biceps and washboard abs? I'm nothing like them. I look like a sorry weakling who couldn't lift a pencil unless it was sharpened. Which is why starting junior high freaked me out.

PE would be different there. You have to change into workout clothes, shower afterward, and change back to regular clothes. In a locker room with all the other guys. What could be more embarrassing for a scrawny guy like me?

I hoped we wouldn't have to dress out right away since the first "week" of school was just two days. But Coach Carter, the PE teacher, passed out school gym uniforms and sent us straight to the locker room the very first class.

I fiddled with my locker combination while the other guys undressed. Everyone was better built than I was—everyone! Some were actually pretty ripped, and the biggest guy looked strong enough to tear our history book apart. There was no way I was showing my wimpy body!

"Man, I feel puky," I told my friend Ben. "I better talk to the coach."

Coach Carter was in the gym, rolling out basketball racks. "Excuse me, sir," I said, "but I don't feel so hot."

He glared at me awhile then finally said, "Go to the nurse's office."

"Yes, sir," I said in a voice as puny as my biceps. "Thank you, sir."

The nurse didn't find anything wrong, of course, but she let me rest the whole period then sent me to my math class. When I slid into the desk next to Ben's, he asked, "Are you OK, Caleb?"

"Yeah, I feel better." But I didn't really. I had only solved my problem for today. Coach Carter wouldn't be fooled again.

But maybe my father would. That evening I limped around for hours. By the time Dad finally noticed and asked what was wrong, I was in actual pain. So I could honestly say, "My ankle really hurts."

"What did you do to it? Maybe you shouldn't participate in PE tomorrow," said Dad.

"I'm not sure what happened. It just hurts." I sighed. "I guess you're right. I better skip PE tomorrow. Could you write me an excuse?"

The coach frowned at the note suspiciously, but my dad has great penmanship so he finally accepted it as authentic. I got to sit on the bleachers and act disappointed that I couldn't play basketball.

When everyone headed to the locker room, the history-book-ripper stopped in front of me and demanded, "What's wrong with you?"

"Sprained ankle," I said.

He looked at his friends. "Aw. Him ankle hurt." They all laughed and walked on.

Ben stopped by, too. "Will you be able to do PE next week?"

I shrugged. "Maybe."

When I got home, I checked the school calendar on the refrigerator. There were 181 days left in the year. It probably wasn't humanly possible to escape PE that many more times, but I had to try. Guys like the Ripper lived to give guys like me a hard time. I couldn't let him or his buddies see my bony chest, flabby gut, and stick-figure arms!

That weekend, I spent hours making a list of ways to get out of PE. By Sunday night, I only had thirty-seven ideas, but hopefully I'd come up with the rest later. I felt bad about being so deceptive, but I told myself I had no choice.

I escaped PE the whole next week by using the first five items on the list:

1. Act sick at the end of art. (That was the class before PE.)
2. Stop at the counselor's office before PE to discuss career possibilities.
3. Volunteer to clean up after art.
4. Wrap knee and convince Dad to write excuse.
5. Involve art teacher in conversation about my newfound passion for painting.

Sometimes I still had to face Coach Carter, but since I always had a note or a late pass, he couldn't do anything but scowl at me.

Friday after school, the Ripper and his gang strode up to my locker. "You're always getting out of PE," said the big guy. "What kind of wuss are you?"

Ben stepped forward. "He's not a wuss at all."

"Yeah!" I peeped.

The Ripper snorted. "Right." Then the final bell sounded, and he and his toadies stomped to the exit.

"Thanks," I told Ben.

"No problem," he said. "See you Monday!"

But on Monday I used the sixth idea on my list which involved a thermometer and my bedside lamp. I felt guilty about tricking Dad again, but what else could I do?

Ben called at lunchtime. "Are you sick?"

I tried to sound weak—which wasn't much of a stretch for me. "Yeah. Real sick."

"Come on, Caleb. What's really going on?"

"I'm sick!" I cried. "I have a fever and everything."

"Uh-huh," he said. "Well . . . see you tomorrow. Right?"

I coughed. "Maybe."

After he hung up, I got out my list. Stretching number six out awhile would really help, but what if Dad took me to the doctor? I decided to move on to the seventh idea.

But when I asked the art teacher to critique a painting after class on Tuesday, she snapped, "Go to PE, Caleb." That told me she was on to me, and I could forget ideas fourteen, twenty-one, and twenty-seven. Then she added, "Don't stop anywhere. Coach Carter is expecting you."

My heart dropped. Was I was totally busted?

The coach didn't speak to me when I walked into the gym, but his laser stare said everything. He watched me like a hawk until I passed through the locker room door. I knew I might as well pitch my whole list.

But I wasn't giving up the fight just yet! I stalled around in the bathroom until things got quiet. When I came out, the Ripper was still there, admiring himself in the long mirror near the showers.

I ducked behind a divider and watched while he flexed his muscles and posed like a bodybuilder. Finally he dropped his arms and just stared at his reflection with this disgusted look on his face.

I knew that expression because I'd seen it on myself before—like every time I looked at myself in a mirror. Did the Ripper hate his body, too? Was that even possible?

"Wuss!" he hissed. For a moment I thought he'd spotted me, but then I realized he was talking to himself. Still, I went back to the bathroom to be safe. I ran some water and then returned to the locker room with loud footsteps. I was alone.

I plopped onto a bench to think. I couldn't believe the most muscular guy around was dissatisfied with his body. And if he felt like that, then how many of the other guys felt the same way? Lots of them probably worried about their bodies just as much as I did!

But I was the only one lying his way out of PE. I'd deceived Dad, the nurse, my teachers—and Ben, too. Sometimes I'd lied to several of them in a single day. At that rate, I could do 181 wrong things before the school year was even halfway over. I didn't want to be that kind of person! And God didn't want that for me either, did he?

So I wasn't happy with the body God gave me! My scrawny outside wasn't all there was to me. God made me a whole person—and I wanted to be a good one. That meant the way I looked at things had to change. I had to treat people—including myself—the right way.

I still hated the idea of undressing in the locker room, but if everybody figured out a way to get through it, then I guess I could just make the best of it too. I was through with schemes! But maybe I would make myself a new list—a plan for getting my body into better shape. And the first step would be to change clothes and go to PE.

Discussion Questions

1. Our faith encourages us to have a positive body image. Why?

2. How often do you judge others by their physical appearances? Why is it wrong to do so?

3. Who or what has the most negative influence on your body image? Who or what has the most positive influence?

4. What methods are used to make models, actors, and celebrities seem perfect? Why?

5. How can you help others feel positive about their bodies? How can you help yourself when you're feeling unattractive in some way?

Activity

Make a poster that uses images and words to encourage other teens to accept and appreciate their bodies as they are.

Prayer

Lord, I know my body is an amazing gift from you, but sometimes it's hard to appreciate that. When I compare myself to other people—in my life and in the media—I start thinking I'm not attractive enough. I worry that my body is flawed, and I focus on finding its imperfections. Please help me accept my body as you made it and love it as it is. Amen.

The Message

God made us in his own image by blessing us with immortal souls, but he also gave us the wonderful gift of our physical bodies. It can be hard to appreciate your body in a culture that overemphasizes appearance. (Almost everyone suffers a negative body image at some time or another!) Here are some ways to boost your self-image and learn to love the body God gave you:

- Make a list of things you like about your body. Read it over daily and add to it as often as you can.
- Try a new sport, craft, or other physical activity. It'll help you appreciate what your body can do.
- Take care of your body by eating right, exercising, getting enough sleep, and keeping clean.
- Establish a rule that any time you think something critical about your body you must compliment yourself, too.
- Your body could change a lot in the next few years. Look at old family photos for proof!
- Fast forward through commercials and flip past magazine ads. Why compare yourself to fake images of unreal perfection?
- Thank God for your body every day!

SUCCESS

THE ISSUE

Internet Pornography

Cyberbullying

Modesty

Family

Materialism

Dishonesty

Body Image

Success

Depression

Substance Abuse

THE FACTS

Many teens today feel tremendous pressure to achieve. Some of that comes from external sources like parents or teachers, but kids often expect too much of themselves. They believe they must excel in every area of life: school, sports, work, friendships, etc. The quest for success can leave teens overscheduled, overworked, and over-stressed. In the past few decades, free time for kids has decreased significantly while time spent in structured sports has doubled and studying has increased by 50 percent. Teens are spending less time on family interaction, church experiences, and unstructured activities than ever before, and many report high levels of stress. Overwhelmed kids often suffer sleep problems, poor eating habits, sports injuries, low self-esteem, and depression. They are also more likely to exaggerate or lie about their achievements.

SCRIPTURE

"Come to me, all you that are weary and are carrying heavy burdens, and I will give you rest."

Matthew 11:28

Save me, O God, for the waters have come up to my neck.

Psalm 69:1

CATECHISM

Just as God "rested on the seventh day from all his work which he had done" (Genesis 2:2), human life has a rhythm of work and rest. The institution of the Lord's Day helps everyone enjoy adequate rest and leisure to cultivate their familial, cultural, social, and religious lives.

CCC no. 2184

Going Under

I was swimming underwater, gliding past beautiful sea plants and colorful fish. When I needed a breath, I headed for the surface, but I swam and swam without ever reaching it. My heart pounded. My lungs burned. Finally I was forced to inhale and . . .

I woke up, gasping and moaning. Every night for a week, I'd had that same nightmare, so I knew what came next: lying awake for hours, stressing over tomorrow's busy schedule.

See, I was drowning in real life, too. Every day was crammed with schoolwork and activities and lessons—and pressure! My parents expected me to be the best at everything, but it's hard to excel when you're exhausted.

Maybe that was why things started falling apart the next day. In first period, I confused Tyler and Taylor on our presidents test. When I told my friend Cass about what an idiot I'd been, she teased, "Oh, no, Aubrey. Now you'll never get into Harvard. Your parents will be crushed."

Mom and Dad actually did worry about how my actions today might affect getting accepted at a good college later. So I didn't find Cass's joke amusing. "Funny," I snapped. "Let's get to class."

The rest of the morning was a wreck, too. When I recited "Casey at the Bat" in English, I forgot a whole stanza. In art, I blotched my ink drawing and had to start over. And in math, I realized too late that I'd skipped half the homework problems. Didn't she say one through forty *odd*?

I couldn't do anything right in my afternoon classes either—or after school. In the middle of French club, I realized I was supposed to be at volleyball practice. The coach didn't say anything when I dashed in late, but I played so poorly she probably wished I'd never shown up.

Then it was my piano lesson . . . home . . . a little supper . . . a lot of homework . . . and bed.

Even though I was worn out, I couldn't sleep. And I was too wound up to pray. I kept thinking about how disappointed my parents would be if they knew about today. Hey, I was disappointed with myself!

I don't usually get emotional, but I cried myself to sleep that evening. Not that I got much rest. The drowning dream haunted me all night. I guess it was my brain's way of telling me I was overwhelmed. Like I didn't already know that!

The next morning, Dad drove me to school for an early community service club meeting. "How are things going?" he asked as we backed out of the driveway.

I knew what he wanted to hear. "Great! I'm working on an interesting science report." I talked about Marie Curie the whole trip so he couldn't question me about anything else.

But as I got out of the car, he asked, "Are you OK? You seem tired."

I almost started crying again, but I controlled myself and said, "I'm fine. See you!" A tear trickled out as I walked off, but I waited until I got inside to wipe it away.

At the meeting, everyone thought I should

handle our next nursing home visit. I wanted to say no, but how could I?

Afterward, at the lockers, Cass took one look at me and demanded, "What's wrong?"

Suddenly I was crying again! What was the matter with me? Cass steered me to the bathroom and handed me tissues until I was cried out. Then I told her about the drowning nightmares and my overwhelming life.

"You need to cut back," she said.

"I can't! I have to keep my grades up. And my clubs and teams need me. Everybody's counting on me." I sighed. "Especially my parents. I can't let them down."

"Tell them you're . . . you know . . . under water."

"Ha ha," I said. "You know, their perfect daughter is not supposed to be a quitter."

"You are so not perfect," she said with a smile.

"I know that!" I shot back. But shouldn't I try to get as close as possible? God would always love me even if I missed the mark. And so would my parents. Still, everybody wanted me to live up to my potential—including me!

After another unsuccessful day and exhausting night, I decided to try Cass's suggestion. At breakfast, I casually said, "I was thinking about giving up the school magazine. I could use some more study time."

"But the magazine is such a good experience," said Dad. That meant it could affect my future (didn't everything?), and he didn't want me to quit.

"Why do you need to study more?" asked Mom. "Are your grades falling?"

"No, they're good." I hoped! "And I want to keep them that way."

"So do we," said Dad.

They launched into a lecture about being excellent or achieving greatness or something—I didn't listen. And I didn't mention dropping activities again. It was obvious they didn't want me to cut anything so what was the point in talking about it? I didn't want to disappoint my parents.

But less than a week later, I let them down anyway. And Cass, too.

In one horrible day, I flunked a social studies quiz, missed the deadline for my science report because I lost it who-knew-where, and found out I only had a B average in math, a subject my parents considered essential for success.

Worst of all, I got cut from the volleyball team! The coach pulled me aside at lunch and told me really nicely, but I still felt terrible. My parents would be so upset. (Playing sports is a good experience, you know.)

After the coach left, I ran to the bathroom and fell apart. Again! Obviously I did not have what it took to truly excel. I was never going to measure up to my parents' expectations. Never.

"Aubrey?" Cass was outside the stall.

I blew my nose and opened the door. "I'm OK."

"Really? It looks to me like you're still in over your head."

I was so tired of her treating my problems like a joke! "You're a terrible friend, you know that?" I shouted. "Just stay out of my life from now on!"

I glimpsed her hurt expression in the mirror as I stomped out. It was too bad our friendship had to end like this, but it was for the best. I didn't have time for a social life anyway!

Later, she caught up with me at my locker. "Listen," she said, "if you actually were drowning in the ocean, you wouldn't refuse help, would you? No! Because you'd know you couldn't save yourself. So talk to your parents and—"

"I tried that already!" I yelled.

"Try again! They love you, Aubrey. I bet they'll ease up once they really understand." She sighed. "You can't go on all stressed out like this."

I knew she was right. The pressure was tearing me apart. Something had to change—and soon!

"I'm sorry I teased you," she went on. "You don't usually get emotional and I didn't know how to handle it, so I made stupid jokes. But I really do care, OK?" She walked off.

How could she reach out to me after I dumped her over a few irritating remarks? I had been a terrible friend to Cass, but that didn't stop her from caring about me anyway!

My parents cared, too. Sure, they stressed about raising me right and that made them demanding sometimes. But they'd love me even if I did disappoint them. And God would, too. So, the thought hit me, who was I trying to be so perfect for? Why was I running myself ragged? Could it be I was pressuring *myself*?

I really needed to think about that sometime, but right now I was going to apologize to Cass. Tonight I'd explain my messed-up life to Mom and Dad. They'd freak at first, but in the end I knew I could count on their help. And I felt ready to accept it—now that I understood I can't rescue myself!

Discussion Questions

1. How did the characters in this story respond to stress? How do you react under pressure?

2. What's the good side of being a high achiever? What's the down side?

3. We're often pushed to excel, but are there times when it would be better to stop pushing so hard? Explain your answer.

4. What does our faith teach us about rest and relaxation, success and achievement? What's your favorite way to de-stress?

5. How can you use your time to reflect your priorities in life?

6. Do you ever pressure someone else? Who, and why?

Activity

Interview someone you consider successful. Ask for advice about setting priorities, budgeting time, and handling stress. Do you think that success automatically leads to happiness?

Prayer

Lord God, sometimes I'm overwhelmed by my busy life.
There are so many things I want to do, so many things I feel
I should do, so many expectations I want to fulfill, so many
demands on my time and energy. I can be my harshest critic,
focusing on my imperfections and falling prey to self-doubt.
Thank you for loving me as I am. Help me balance my life, cope with
stress, and set priorities based on the values of my faith. Amen.

The Message

Everybody experiences stress—it's part of life. But maybe you're feeling too much pressure. High expectations from parents and teachers, full schedules, social demands, and your own desire to excel can bring you down and burn you out. Follow the suggestions below to get some balance in your life and control stress:

- Make a list of your activities in order from most to least important. Drop one or more activities from the bottom of the list.

- Whenever possible, match the time you spend on an activity to its importance. In other words, spend most of your time on what really matters.

- Set time limits on open-ended activities like studying for a test.

- Allow yourself "time off" to relax, have fun with friends, or just veg out.

- Be healthy. Eat good foods, avoid too much caffeine, get plenty of sleep, and do some noncompetitive physical activity.

- Don't compare yourself to others. It may seem like they're achieving so much more than you are, but they're probably overstressed, too.

- Several times a day, take a moment to stop everything and focus on God. Say a prayer or just feel his presence in silence.

- Have an honest conversation with your parents about your potential and their expectations.

Internet Pornography

Cyberbullying

Modesty

DEPRESSION

THE ISSUE

family

Materialism

Dishonesty

Body Image

Success

Depression

Substance Abuse

THE FACTS

At any one time, 10–15 percent of teens are depressed, according to recent studies. Research also shows that 20 percent of teens will experience depression before they reach adulthood. Traumatic events such as death, accident, or illness can cause depression in teens, but the condition can also be triggered by irregular brain chemistry, genetic tendencies, seasonal changes, ongoing social problems, or life's "normal" changes and stresses. Sometimes depression seems to have no definite cause at all, but even so, it is a serious condition. Unfortunately, most depressed teens don't get help because the symptoms of teen depression are often missed by adults or passed off as typical teenage behavior. Without treatment, depression can lead to problems like trouble in school, relationship issues, substance abuse, risky sexual behaviors, and suicide, which is the third leading cause of death for teens. Most depressed teens can be helped with therapy and/or medication and go on to live normal lives.

SCRIPTURE

The Lord is near to the brokenhearted, and saves the crushed in spirit.

Psalm 34:18

Cast all your anxiety on him, because he cares for you.

1 Peter 5:7

"Peace I leave with you; my peace I give to you. I do not give to you as the world gives. Do not let your hearts be troubled, and do not let them be afraid."

John 14:27

CATECHISM

The Beatitudes respond to the natural desire for happiness. This desire is of divine origin: God has placed it in the human heart in order to draw man to the One who alone can fulfill it:

> We all want to live happily; in the whole human race there is no one who does not assent to this proposition, even before it is fully articulated.

> How is it, then, that I seek you, Lord? Since in seeking you, my God, I seek a happy life, let me seek you so that my soul may live, for my body draws life from my soul and my soul draws life from you.

> God alone satisfies.

CCC no. 1718

Chapter 9

In the Shadows

At first, I didn't notice Marshall was changing. What a great friend, huh? If I'd only paid attention, I might have spotted the problem sooner—like when we did the youth group fundraiser.

Marshall and I usually competed over stuff like that, but he didn't even try to sell any popcorn. "Sheesh," I said one day. "Are you just going to *let* me win?"

"Of course not, Shea," he replied. "Fundraising is my life, you know."

I had to laugh at that. Who could blame him if he was tired of selling stuff after all these years? Besides, Marshall cared about what really mattered. There was nobody in our group who was more into service than that guy.

I dropped the issue, but I did outsell everybody. For my reward, I got to cream-pie our sponsor, Mr. Emilio. A newspaper photographer took a picture of the moment.

"I never thought I'd be news," I told Marshall afterward. "How cool is that?"

"Pretty cool." He didn't seem that excited, but I talked about the photo for days.

Then there was the election in homeroom. Five of us were nominated for student council. Marshall and the others gave serious speeches, but I just said, "Lunch lines—too long! Lunch period—too short! Let's stop the madness, people." Everybody applauded, and I got elected.

"I cannot believe I won," I told Marshall as we headed to the buses.

"It's amazing all right," he replied.

"Funny. You know why people voted for me?" I went on to analyze my success.

A week later, the winners of the Columbus Day essay contest were announced at an assembly, and I received honorable mention. When I returned to my seat, I showed my ribbon to Marshall and, I hate to say it, started bragging.

"Uh-huh," he said dully. "You rock."

That's when I finally realized something was wrong. A lot of good stuff had happened to me, but it seemed like Marshall couldn't care less. We were good friends. What was up?

After that, I noticed Marshall wasn't as talkative as he used to be. He didn't really listen when I talked either. And sometimes he had lame reasons for not doing stuff. Working on a service project was OK, but finishing chores or taking a nap didn't cut it as excuses.

Could it be he was bothered by my winning streak? Our friendly competition had never caused problems before, but things usually worked out pretty evenly. I'd been outshining Marshall a lot lately. Maybe he just didn't want to live in my shadow.

Yeah, he must be jealous, I thought. Well, he wouldn't hold a grudge for long. If I just waited, things would soon return to normal.

Instead, the situation got worse! Marshall didn't show up for basketball tryouts, and he ignored all my texts about it. When I questioned him at the lockers the next morning, he just shrugged and said, "I'm not playing basketball this year."

"But the team needs you!"

"There are plenty of better players," he said. "Like you. You'll be a real asset to the team." He started digging through his locker like the conversation was over.

Was he afraid I'd outdo him again? Probably, but Marshall *loved* basketball. He had to be feeling really bad about himself if he was willing to sit out the season.

Had my accomplishments shaken his confidence that much? Of course, there was nothing wrong with succeeding, but I did have a tendency to gloat. I must have made him feel like a complete loser. Now he was too down on himself to play his favorite sport—and it was my fault.

I felt sorry about that, but I figured I could fix things. I just had to build him back up. "You're a good player, Marsh," I told him. "You'd be valuable to the team, too."

"Thanks," he said, "but I'm really not up for it. I'll just drag the team down if I play."

He was dragging me down already, but I was determined to cheer him up. It was only right since I was sort of responsible for his low self-esteem.

For the next couple of weeks, I said supportive stuff whenever I could. And I kept asking Marshall to do things even though he almost always said no. I even prayed for him.

But he just seemed to sink lower and lower. He quit doing his schoolwork. He barely answered when anybody spoke to him. And he dragged around like he was half-asleep. It seemed like he'd never stop the downhill slide. Maybe I was partly to blame.

Then something hopeful finally happened! Mr. Emilio announced someone in youth group had won the Saint Vincent Award from the diocese. "It's given to a young person who lives the Gospel through service to others," he said. "And this year the award goes to Marshall."

As the room exploded with applause and cheers, I realized this was just the boost Marshall needed! Winning a service award was more meaningful than all of my recent accomplishments put together. He didn't have to feel inferior anymore.

When we were waiting for our rides afterward, I said, "That award is really a big deal."

"Yeah," he said. "How did somebody like me ever win something like that?"

I couldn't believe it! His attitude hadn't changed at all. "Look," I said, "I understand how you got down on yourself to start out. It's not easy to see somebody else succeeding when you're . . . um . . . not. And I shouldn't have rubbed it in like I did. But this is so—"

"Not everything is about you, Shea," he snapped. "So just leave me alone." He trotted across the parking lot to his dad's car.

At that moment, I was totally fed up with Marshall, but later, just before I went to bed, I decided to pray for him anyway. He really needed God's help. So did I. *Please, Lord*, I prayed. *Guide me. I don't know what to do about this mess I made.*

I didn't have to deal with Marshall at school the next day because he was absent. But that evening he showed up at my door and asked, "Can I talk to you?" When I nodded, he came in, sat down, and blurted out, "I'm depressed, Shea. I mean . . . I'm suffering from actual depression." He explained he'd had the problem awhile—like long before my winning streak.

"I . . . I'm sorry," I said. "How could I have missed it?"

"I've been covering up," he told me. "I didn't want anybody to know I was struggling—including my parents. I thought I could handle it myself. But things kept getting worse and worse."

"Yeah," I said quietly. "I did notice that."

"Last night I realized you thought my problems were your fault," he said. "So I decided I had to tell you what was really going on and make you understand that depression just happens sometimes. It's like something's out of balance in your body. You need professional help to handle it. You know . . . like therapy. And maybe medication."

"Are you getting help like that?" I asked.

"I am now. Which doesn't mean I'm suddenly cured, OK? Depression could be a challenge I always have to live with. So stop blaming yourself. You didn't cause my problems. And you can't solve them."

That was a relief, but I still felt bad for Marshall. I thought I had cast this huge shadow over him, but he had been struggling in real darkness. No wonder my lame attempts to fix things didn't work!

"Thanks for telling me," I said. "I wish I could help."

"You can," he replied in a joking tone I hadn't heard in a while. "Quit trying to cheer me up, OK? Please." Then he got serious. "And just be my friend."

So that's what I've been doing lately. It's not always easy to handle Marshall's situation, but I'm hanging in there. He's making progress, I can tell, and I believe one day he'll be able to deal with his depression in a better way. With God's help. And my friendship, too.

Discussion Questions

1. Why do you think so many people in our society suffer depression?

2. How can faith help you cope when you're feeling down?

3. Why do people who suffer depression try to hide it? Why is this a bad way to handle the problem?

4. If it's difficult to get help at home, where else could a troubled person turn?

5. What are some ways you can help a depressed friend?

Activity

Even the saints suffered discouragement and depression. (Check out Saint Dymphna or Saint John Vianney). Research a saint whose struggles inspire you personally. Prepare and perform a monologue about the saint's life to encourage others.

Prayer

Be with me, God, in times of hopelessness and discouragement, and give me the insight to see when others are suffering in darkness, too. Guide me as I seek help for myself or anyone else in despair. Bring us all closer to you, and help us find contentment in lives of faith and service. Amen.

The Message

Everyone feels down sometimes, but depression is more serious than a bad mood or a negative attitude. Depression can have a devastating effect on people's lives, and most sufferers cannot address it without help. How can you tell if someone in your life is depressed? Watch for the following signs:

- Feelings of sadness, emptiness, or hopelessness lasting more than two weeks;
- Pulling away from family and friends;
- Trouble at school or work;
- Losing interest in things;
- Consistently being bored or unmotivated;
- Extreme habits like sleeping too much or not enough, not eating or overeating, lack of emotion or overreaction;

- Inability to enjoy life;
- Low self-esteem;
- Forgetfulness, poor concentration, failure to fulfill responsibilities;
- Physical complaints like stomach pain, headaches, lack of energy;
- Substance abuse.

Remember: a depressed person needs help. While your support can mean a lot, it's important to involve professionals.

Internet Pornography
Cyberbullying
Modesty
Family
Materialism
Dishonesty
Body Image
Success
Depression
Substance Abuse

SUBSTANCE ABUSE

THE ISSUE

THE FACTS

Chapter 10

Substance abuse is a problem for millions of teens. In recent years, studies have shown that 9–11 percent of teens turn to drugs like marijuana, hallucinogens, cocaine, inhalants, and prescription medications. The statistics for alcohol abuse are even more alarming, with 15 percent or more of teens currently drinking regularly. Many of those teens engage in binge drinking, consuming five or more alcoholic drinks on a single occasion. Substance abuse can affect school performance, damage relationships with family and friends, cause physical problems, and lead to other high-risk behaviors. When surveyed, most teens say they know other kids who use drugs or alcohol and they disapprove. However, few teens report their peers since doing so is perceived as betrayal.

SCRIPTURE

Two are better than one, because they have a good reward for their toil. For if they fall, one will lift up the other; but woe to one who is alone and falls and does not have another to help.

Ecclesiastes 4:9–10

Do not get drunk with wine, for that is debauchery; but be filled with the Spirit.

Ephesians 5:18

CATECHISM

The virtue of temperance disposes us to *avoid every kind of excess*: the abuse of food, alcohol, tobacco, or medicine. Those incur grave guilt who, by drunkenness or a love of speed, endanger their own and others' safety on the road, at sea, or in the air.

CCC no. 2290

THE STORY

Not My Sister

My older sister and I have our problems, of course. We argue; we tease; we play pranks; we "borrow" stuff; we complain. You know . . . we act like sisters.

Except for one thing. We don't believe in telling on each other. Some of my friends and their sisters get each other into trouble all the time, but to Megan and me, sisters don't snitch on sisters. Ever.

So when I caught her tiptoeing upstairs after curfew one night, I didn't even think about ratting her out. I just followed her into her room, shut the door, and said, "You're late."

"I know that, Ava," she said. "We lost track of the time, OK? Elle drove me home as soon as we realized." She flopped onto her bed. "Now go away, and let me get some sleep."

Breaking curfew once didn't seem like a big deal, so I let it go. But then Megan did it again. And again.

"I'm just hanging out with friends," she said when I questioned her the last time. "You're not going to tell Mom and Dad, are you?"

How could she even ask? "No! But what are you doing? I'm concerned. It's not safe to be out so late."

Her face relaxed. "That's nice, but there's nothing to worry about."

A few nights later, I woke up to my sister shouting. From what I could tell from eavesdropping at my door, Mom and Dad had caught Megan sneaking in. She argued and argued that she'd lost track of the time and didn't deserve to be punished, but they grounded her anyway.

After everything was over, I slipped into Megan's room. I couldn't believe it when she whirled around and hissed, "What kind of sister are you—selling me out like that?"

"I didn't say anything!" I cried. "I would never do that to you."

"I'm . . . I'm sorry, Ava," she said. "I know you wouldn't. But it was like they were lying in wait for me, so I guess I just got suspicious." Before I could ask how she could suspect her own sister, she added, "Hey, you better return to your cell before the wardens catch you."

I went back to bed, but I couldn't sleep. Megan seemed to be changing, and that bothered me. It wasn't like her to break major rules or to yell at our parents. And I never thought she'd ever doubt me—not my sister! Whatever was going on with her, I had to prove she could still rely on me.

I got the chance to do that a week later. After school, I found Megan getting sick in the bathroom we shared. I held her hair for her then got her a damp cloth when she finished. "You'd better lie down," I told her. "I'll call Mom and see if she can come home early."

"No!" she cried. "You can't say anything about this."

"But you're sick, and you—"

"I just had a little too much to drink, but now I'm OK." She rolled her eyes and added, "Don't look so shocked. People drink all the time, you know. And there's nothing wrong with having a few drinks with friends. I overdid it this time, but believe me, I won't again."

60

Plenty of people drank—I knew that. But Megan was underage. Still as long as she kept it under control, I guessed it wasn't really a big problem, right? "OK then," I said with a sigh. "Just be careful."

"Thanks, Sis. I knew I could count on you."

I went to my room and lay on my bed to think. How long had Megan been drinking? Was that why she broke curfew? Did she and her friends drink at school today?

After a while I decided there was no point in worrying about any of that. It wasn't like I could do anything about it . . . except tell my parents. And even though I felt bad for keeping secrets from Mom and Dad, I'd never squeal on my own sister. Never.

For a while afterward, Megan acted like her old self, getting along with our parents and obeying her curfew once she got ungrounded. All of which confirmed that it was right for me to keep quiet. Betraying my sister would have been wrong, of course, but it also would have upset Mom and Dad for no good reason.

One Saturday afternoon, Megan came to my room and handed me her favorite purple sweater. "I know you love it, and now it's yours."

"Thanks!" I slipped the sweater on over my tee. "How's it look?"

"Fantastic!" She started to leave then turned back. "Hey, can I borrow some cash? We're having a little party at Elle's tonight, and I have to chip in for the drinks."

My heart sank. "Drinks? Like *alcohol*?"

Megan laughed. "It wouldn't be a party otherwise. Don't worry. I'll take it easy."

"I guess a few drinks never hurt anybody, but Mom and Dad would freak if they knew you were breaking the law."

"They won't find out." Her eyes flicked to the sweater then back to my face. "*Right*?"

It felt awful to think that she still didn't trust me to be a good sister. "Not from me!" I cried, grabbing my purse and giving her some money.

"Thanks," she said. "You're the best!"

After she left, I couldn't help but wonder . . . was she trying to buy me off? Sisters don't bribe sisters—not if they have a good relationship. I put the sweater away in a drawer. Wearing it would only remind me how much things had changed between Megan and me.

She might have forgotten what it meant to be sisters, but I hadn't. I probably would have kept her secret forever. And anyway . . . it wasn't like her drinking did any harm. Or that's what I kept telling myself.

Until the day I walked into the bathroom and saw Megan gulping down cough syrup. I was so stunned I just stood there and watched her finish off the bottle.

She frowned when she saw me. "What's that look for? I have a cough, OK? And I'm taking medicine."

"You're only supposed to use a spoonful. That medicine has alcohol in it."

"Don't make a big deal out of nothing!" She turned away and started brushing her teeth.

I knew people didn't do stuff like guzzle cough medicine unless they had real issues with alcohol. How could I have not realized Megan had such a serious problem? What kind of sister doesn't notice a thing like that?

Maybe Megan was really good at covering up. Or maybe I focused so much on how she hurt my feelings that I didn't pay enough attention. Maybe I just didn't *want* to see the problem. I made so many excuses for Megan's behavior, even pretending it didn't matter that she was doing something illegal. I just couldn't admit that my sister was willing to do anything for alcohol—deceive our parents, break the law, take risks—anything.

Well, I couldn't avoid the truth any longer. Megan was abusing alcohol—and I'd been helping her get away with it!

Tears came to my eyes, but I managed to choke out, "You have a problem, Megan. And you need help."

She spun around, her face full of anger.

"I . . . I have to tell," I hiccupped.

Megan exploded, calling me a traitor and some dirty names, too. Finally, she screamed, "If you snitch, then you're not my sister anymore!" Then she ran downstairs and out of the house.

For the next couple of hours, I cried and prayed, asking God to help me do what I had to do. When Mom and Dad got home, I told them everything. Of course, they were upset about how I covered for Megan, but their big concern was getting her the help she needed.

My sister's in rehab now, and my family will start counseling soon. Megan didn't speak to me at all before she left. It hurts so much to know she hates me. I just pray that one day she realizes I told on her for her own good. And if she doesn't . . . well . . . I'll always be there for her anyway. Because sisters never give up on sisters. Never.

Discussion Questions

1. Jesus said, "No one can serve two masters" (Matthew 6:24). He was talking about God and wealth, but how could this passage apply to substance abuse?

2. What's the difference between using a substance and abusing it?

3. What do you think leads someone to abuse alcohol or drugs?

4. When should you tell on someone or reveal a secret? Who should you tell?

5. Some people feel that telling on someone is always a betrayal. Do you agree? Why or why not?

Activity

Sometimes the media represents drinking and other substance use in an unrealistic and even positive way. Rewrite a commercial or a movie scene to show the truth, and act it out with your friends.

Prayer

Lord, help me recognize when others are in trouble,
especially if they are dealing with drug and alcohol problems.
Give me the courage to seek help for those in need
even in the face of their anger and rejection.
Keep me free from substance abuse myself,
and bless me with a clear mind and a healthy body.
Amen.

The Message

Many people who misuse drugs or alcohol manage to hide their problems from family and friends. How can you tell if someone in your life is abusing substances? Look for these signs:

- Changes in personality such as becoming unsociable, turning moody or angry, seeming depressed, or otherwise acting unlike his/her usual self;

- Frequent sickness, red or dilated eyes, fatigue, or other physical issues;

- New problems at school, work, or other activities such as poor attendance, underachievement, lack of responsibility, or conflicts with others;

- Loss of interest in hobbies or other previously enjoyed activities;

- Avoiding or dropping old friends;

- Increased trouble getting along with family;

- Lying, stealing, sneaking around, and other deceptive behaviors.

Substance abuse issues can't be handled alone!

More Ideas for Activities

A wrap-up activity is suggested in each chapter of this book, but you might prefer to select from the list below. When assigning your chosen activity, add a specific focus to the project so it relates to the current chapter. For example, the goal of the first task below could be to discourage substance abuse, speak out against bullying, or suggest a good way to de-stress, depending on the topic.

Media

Post a message on social media.

Film your own movie.

Start a website or blog.

Create an advertising campaign.

Redo a commercial.

Writing

Write a letter to a story character, a friend, a younger student, or your future self.

Select a scripture passage, and explain what the verse means to you.

Keep a journal.

Write a story, essay, poem, or article.

Make a top ten list.

Theater

Role play.

Act out the current chapter's story as it is or with a changed ending.

Stage a mock trial, news program, or talk show.

Write and present a play, skit, dialogue, or monologue.

Hold an "open mike" night at your church or school.

Other Arts

Decorate a button or t-shirt with a message.

Work with others to create a mural.

Write and perform a song.

Make a drawing, painting, sculpture, or collage.

Create a thought-provoking and/or educational board game.

Research

Prepare for and participate in a debate.

Read a book and report on it orally or in writing.

Collect information through surveys, observation, or online communication and display your results graphically.

Research a person or topic and write a report.

Interview someone.

Sharing

Put up a bulletin board in a public area.

Plan and carry out a service project.

Make and send an encouraging greeting card.

Present one of your projects to younger kids.

Communicate with other teens using posters or banners.

Miscellaneous

Invite a knowledgeable person to give a talk.

Plan a field trip.

Write a prayer.

Dress up and assume someone else's identity for an interview, "wax museum," or other special program.

Write, illustrate, and put together a comic book, pop-up book, or child's picture book.

How Can I Help?

If you know another teen who's dealing with any kind of serious problem, you're probably concerned and you may wish you could help. But what can you do for someone who's engaging in risky or self-destructive behavior, or choosing a path you know is wrong? Here are some suggestions:

Put it out there. You might feel uncomfortable bringing the problem up, but you need to try. In a conversation or letter, tell what you've observed and admit you're concerned. Listen if the other person wants to talk.

Keep at it. If your friend or family member denies that there's a problem or refuses to talk, say that you care and that you're willing to listen anytime he/she wants. Then try to restart the conversation at a later time.

Respect the problem. If your friend or family member decides to share with you, treat his/her concerns seriously. Don't act like things can be fixed easily, compare the problem to worse situations, or make "cheerful" remarks.

Encourage the person to take action. If the situation isn't urgent, try to get the other person to seek help from an adult. Volunteer to be there when it happens.

Take immediate action if needed. If you think anyone is in danger of getting hurt, you *must* tell an adult who can help—even if your friend or family member becomes angry at you for doing it. Talk to your parents, your friend's parents, a teacher, your pastor, or another adult you trust.

Do something together. Keeping busy can give us a break from life's problems and help relieve stress. If your friend or family member isn't interested in your usual activities, suggest some light exercise like taking a walk or another tension-reliever like listening to music.

Stand by the other person. Your friend or family member's social life might suffer because he/she is acting differently. Eat lunch together, hang out after school, or do whatever you normally do. Showing you're still willing to be close might influence others to be more understanding—and it will mean a lot to the person who is troubled.

Pray. Your friend or family member needs your prayers, of course, but he/she might also be willing to pray *with* you. If that's not something you find easy to do together, try traditional prayers you know by heart like the "Our Father," or pray the Rosary together. Or promise to pray the same prayer or at the same time separately every day.

Know your limits. Serious problems require serious help that you are not qualified to provide. Never keep dangerous secrets or try to solve the other person's issues yourself. Doing so only keeps your friend from getting the adult involvement, professional therapy, medical intervention, or other help that's needed. Don't risk being overwhelmed yourself. Just concentrate on being a good friend.

A Letter to Parents

Dear Parents,

Today's young teens will face many challenges before they reach adulthood, and they'll need faith to guide them along the way. But when kids are overwhelmed by negative influences, it's hard for them to live the Catholic principles they've been taught. They need help to see how faith applies to their real lives—and encouragement to follow Christ even in the toughest situations.

That's why I'll be teaching lessons from *Tackling Tough Topics with Faith and Fiction*. This faith-based resource book uses realistic stories about contemporary teens to show the value of faith in difficult times and sensitive situations. *Tackling Tough Topics with Faith and Fiction* also includes discussion questions, activities, prayers, scripture and catechism references, and practical advice—all designed to help young people grow their faith in preparation for the moral challenges they may encounter.

I am planning to cover the following topics:

I know you share my goal of preparing your child to live a life of faith. You are your child's most influential teacher so your interest and support are important. If you have any questions about this initiative, don't hesitate to contact me at:

Thank you. God bless you and your family.
Sincerely,

Talking with Your Teen

Growing up in today's world isn't easy—and neither is talking with teens about the serious and faith-challenging issues they face. Though your child may seem to pull away from you during these years, your values, opinions, and support still matter—perhaps more than you realize. So, difficult as it may be, it's important that you communicate with your teen. Here are some suggestions to help you do that:

Take advantage of teachable moments. Instead of sitting your teen down for one long talk (read: lecture) about a sensitive topic, watch for multiple appropriate opportunities to discuss things in bite-sized pieces. For example, the same important issue might be raised on a television program or movie, by news events, in a homily, by the actions of a friend, or through lessons at church or school. These are all natural chances for you to ask about your child's thoughts and feelings and examine the subject together in a non-threatening way.

Be real. Honesty is essential for good communication. Admit it when you feel uncomfortable speaking about a particular topic. (But decide not to let your discomfort keep you from talking about it.) Don't pretend you're some kind of expert—on the subject you're discussing or even about life in general. When you don't know something, admit it readily, and tell your teen you'll talk again after you've found out more information or thought things through. And don't pretend to be "cool"—you're not. Just be yourself.

Show respect. Speak privately with your teen—not in front of friends or family. Avoid insulting your child by talking down, belittling his/her problems, discounting friends and their opinions, or claiming you understand what life is like for a teenager *today*. Try not to preach or nag. In fact, don't talk too much at all. Instead, spend most of your discussion time listening respectfully to what your child has to say.

Ask good questions. Gentle questions can keep the conversation going. Try more open-ended questions that can't be answered in a word or two, and really listen to how your child responds. Occasional questions can guide a discussion, but make sure they're genuine. Teens aren't fooled by fake inquiries designed to express adult opinions or manipulate their behavior. ("Don't you think it would be right to . . . ?" "Wouldn't you feel better if you . . . ?")

Exercise self-control. Teens can be emotional so they need you to stay calm. That can be tough, but remember—you are your child's anchor. Think before you speak, and try to be nonjudgmental. Watch your body language! If you sigh, roll your eyes, cross your arms, or frown, your child will feel you disapprove even if you claim to be supportive.

Show you care. Even if you're sure your child knows you love him/her, it helps to say so. The struggles of growing up can sap confidence and make teens feel unlovable. It's particularly important to express your love in times of conflict—that's when your teen needs your support the most! Assure your child of God's love, too. Encourage your teen to pray, and promise to include him/her in your prayers. Try praying together.

About the Author

After over twenty years as a special education teacher, Diana R. Jenkins became a freelance writer. She has written hundreds of magazine stories, articles, and comic strips for kids and teens. Her books include *Goodness Graces! Ten Short Stories about the Sacraments, Saints of Note—The Comic Collection, The Stepping Stones Journals,* and *Spotlight on Saints! A Year of Funny Readers Theatre for Today's Catholic Kids.* Her short stories have been published in several Catholic Quick Reads including *Now You're Cooking! Ten Short Stories with Recipes, Friend 2 Friend—Twelve Short Stories, Family Ties—Thirteen Short Stories,* and *Celebrate the Season! Twelve Short Stories for Advent and Christmas.* She lives in Montgomery, Ohio with her husband, a medical physicist. Visit her on the web at www.dianarjenkins.bravehost.com, read her blog at http://djsthoughts-dj.blogspot.com, and find her on Facebook at www.facebook.com/dianarjenkins.

Who: The Daughters of St. Paul

What: Pauline Teen—linking your life to Jesus Christ and his Church

When: 24/7

Where: All over the world and on www.pauline.org

Why: Because our life-long passion is to witness to God's amazing love for all people!

How: Inspiring lives of holiness through: APPs, digital media, concerts, websites, social media, videos, blogs, books, music albums, radio, media literacy, DVDs, ebooks, stores, conferences, bookfairs, parish exhibits, personal contact, illustration, vocation talks, photography, writing, editing, graphic design, marketing...

Catholic Fiction

Pauline brings your teens books they'll love —and you can trust! We promise you stories that

- uphold and promote a Catholic worldview
- help kids to explore choices and their consequences
- celebrate Christian values and virtues
- understand the challenges teens face following Christ today
- show how to live the faith where you are
- connect real-life issues with Catholic faith

At Pauline, we love a good story and the long tradition of Christian fiction. Our books are fun to read. And the stories will engage your teens' faith by accepting who they are *here and now* while inspiring them to recognize who God *calls them to become*.

Gifts and resources for parents, teachers, and catechists.

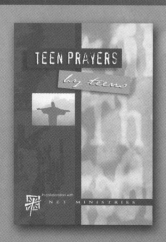

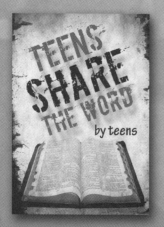

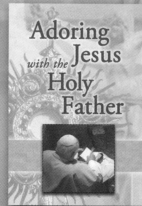

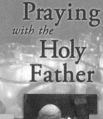

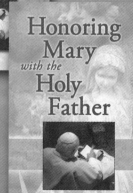

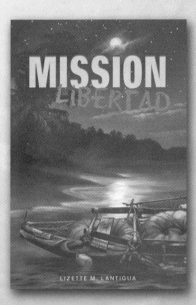

immionation/communism/
adventure

self-acceptance/giftedness/
humor

gifts and limitations/service/
humor

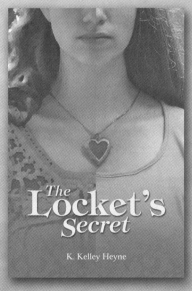

family/fantasy/grief

faith/choices/sex and
relationships

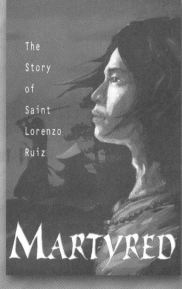

martyrdom/persecution/history